FRONTIER DAYS IN CRESCENTA VALLEY

FRONTIER DAYS IN CRESCENTA VALLEY

PORTRAITS OF LIFE IN THE FOOTHILLS

JO ANNE SADLER

THE History PRESS

Published by The History Press
Charleston, SC 29403
www.historypress.net

Cover images: Front image courtesy of John W. Robinson; back images courtesy of Lanterman Historical Museum Foundation, Timothy MacDonald and John W. Robinson.

First published 2014

Manufactured in the United States

ISBN 978.1.62619.508.0

Library of Congress CIP data applied for.

Contents

ACKNOWLEDGEMENTS

No man is an island, and neither is an author, especially when writing historical books. Again I thank Melissa Patton, director, and Tim Gregory, archivist, at the Lanterman Historical Museum Foundations. Thanks to the Glendale, La Crescenta, Montrose, La Cañada Flintridge and Pasadena Public Libraries; the Southern California Genealogical Library; the Huntington Library Archives; and the Pasadena Museum of History.

Individuals who have generously shared their photographs are Jacqueline Kennedy, Lori Ward Kent, Timothy MacDonald of Beinn Bhreagh Vineyard and John W. Robinson. Thanks to William Lewis of Bill's Bees for graciously giving me a tour of his apiary in Angeles National Forest.

Using primary sources, newspapers and writings of the day gives a voice to the events as they happened, rather than basing the narrative on thirdhand information.

The Historical Society of the Crescenta Valley and its supporters in the past twelve years have generated and inspired many new books about Valley history, and they are to be commended for being such a force in local history.

Unless otherwise noted, photographs and graphics in this book are from the archives of the Historical Society of the Crescenta Valley and the La Cañada Congregational Church photography collection at the Lanterman Historical Museum Archives.

Introduction

This book is a companion to *Crescenta Valley Pioneers and Their Legacies*, which featured the early nineteenth-century settlers who left a permanent imprint on the Crescenta Valley. *Frontier Days* continues the journey and chronicles the challenges of daily life, beekeeping, hunting, major incidents and lost landmarks.

While the Crescenta Valley was not the Wild West, it was a frontier area, a place living on the edge of civilization—in this case, the nearby city of Los Angeles. It was remote, and people looked to one another for support and their social life. Until the Arroyo Seco Bridge was opened in May 1893, even getting to Pasadena necessitated crossing the rugged Arroyo Seco, which could be very dangerous in rainy weather.

In our modern lives, we tend to view the "olden days" through rose-colored glasses, longing for a simpler, less complicated life. While it was a simpler time, it was a much harder life—no welfare net, corner takeout, electricity, refrigeration, telephones, washing machines or 911 assistance. Meat and chicken did not come from the supermarket wrapped in plastic but as a result of hunting and butchering it yourself. Children were born at home, and many died from common childhood illnesses; an appendix attack often resulted in death due to the distance from medical care, and there were no antibiotics, much less penicillin. There was no TV, movies or Internet access—while offering us more diversions, they nonetheless make for a more independent, isolated life today.

Using newspapers and writings of the day, I have attempted to give a realistic view of how people thought and lived. They may have not have been as politically correct as we would like in our modern day, but we cannot look at nineteenth-century people from twenty-first-century viewpoints. We must try to put ourselves in their time and place.

CHAPTER 1

BEE RANCHING AND GREASEWOOD

Making a Living in the Early Days

When the first pioneers settled in the Valley, the land was in a natural state, totally undeveloped and full of native plants, sage, deer, rabbit, quail, bears and lots of rattlesnakes. Much has been written about all the fruit, vineyards and olive groves, but before pioneers could even begin planting, the land needed to be cleared of greasewood and other native plants and a reliable water source secured. Then, after planting their orchards, there was a three- to five-year wait until the groves and grapevines would start to be commercially profitable.

When Henry Hancock surveyed the boundaries of Rancho La Cañada in 1858, he did not venture into the mountains but rather marked them "unsurveyable—good for bees only."

The September 1875 government survey that established the township lines for Township 2N included this general description: "There is a very small proportion of agricultural land in this Township situated along the Northern boundary of the Rancho La Canada. There are settlers along the foot hills who are principally engaged in Bee Culture. The Mountains are high with scattering Timber: Oak, Pine and Fir, the greater portion of which is only Valuable for Fuel."

What did the settlers do to support themselves while waiting for the orchards to start to produce? I am not talking about moneyed men like Adolphus Wesley Williams, Dr. Benjamin B. Briggs and Dr. Jacob Lanterman, each of whom came here with the means to purchase large tracts of land with the intent to subdivide and make a profit, or men like

Thomas Spencer Hall who lived and worked in Los Angeles and developed properties in their spare time. I am talking about the very first "rude forefathers of the hamlet," as Charles Pate called them. These settlers had no plan to fall back on, but they did have families to feed and needed to make a living from day one.

Farming is a seasonal business, always at the mercy of nature; farmers traditionally have had more than one way to earn a living. The early settlers planted quick grain crops—barley for animal fodder, alfalfa for the dairy cows, hay, pumpkins and melons between the newly planted orchards—and hired out with their wagon and team of horses for five dollars per day. They would sell their animal and rattlesnake skins to hide dealers in Los Angeles. The women, like farmwomen everywhere, sold or bartered their excess eggs and milk, would take in laundry and mending, took in boarders and worked in the seasonal harvests and local packing operations.

There was timber harvesting early on, but that involved a more expensive operation of hauling and transporting timber down the mountains to the city of Los Angeles and was financed by moneyed men from Los Angeles. In the early days, for the earliest settlers, there was only greasewood and bee ranching.

GREASEWOOD

One source of income was selling cleared greasewood plants for a few dollars per wagonload for fuel in Los Angeles. In 1885, the Wood-Growers Yard on Los Angeles Street was selling greasewood for seven dollars per cord delivered. Greasewood is a highly flammable native plant that is found in the Southwest and West and is a good source of fuel. The type of greasewood found in Southern California is different than the type in the Southwest and is sometimes incorrectly called sagebrush.

Greasewood is a weedy shrub that can grow up to seven feet tall; is adapted to hot, dry summers; and grows in dry streambeds, canyons and arroyos. It is highly toxic to unadapted animals such as sheep and cattle—even honeybees will not feed from its flowers. It took decades to clear the Valley of greasewood, but it is still here and regrows well after fires. It can have a fifty-foot taproot, often an indicator of a deep water source in the area, but this also makes it a difficult task to clear out.

As a letter from an apiarist noted in the January 9, 1872 *Pacific Rural Press*:

> *There are two plants called greasewood; neither of them being honey plants. One is a bitter, aromatic plant. Like artemesia or wormwood, in odor and taste, but with finely cut leaves. It covers whole mountain sides here in Southern California. It is called "old man" and "sage brush" but it is no more sage than a hog is a sheep. Indians put it on cuts to stop bleeding; it grows in tufts or bunches; some grow three or four feet high. The other kind of greasewood grows more like a bush; has wide leaves, and resembles a kind of chaparral, both are plentiful here. I never knew bees to work on either, but have known them to starve right near it.*

Charles Pate wrote about being out in the pouring rain, gathering wet brush and tramping it into the winter rills to prevent the rushing water from cutting things to pieces.

That greasewood was not only a source of money but also the primary source of fuel in the Valley is reflected in this Crescenta item in the October 3, 1889 *Pasadena Evening News*: "Wagons continue to go out of our valley with the grease-roots of commerce. When the supply is exhausted where shall we look for our fuel? Shall we mine for coal in the distant hills, or shall we plant eucalyptus to be cut down for fuel?"

The July 2009 *Historical Society of the Crescenta Valley Ledger* reprinted an interview of Herbert Bathey by Grace Carpenter of the *Crescenta Valley Ledger* in the 1960s, noting, "The land was gradually cleared of the old, high grease brush that covered the Valley, as crews of whites, chinks, and Mexes and others cut it for fuel. There was a large wood market on Los Angeles street between 1st and Aliso."

BEE RANCHES

There are certain pursuits which, if not wholly poetic and true, do at least suggest a nobler and finer relation to nature than we know. The keeping of bees, for instance.

—Henry David Thoreau

The industry that has been largely ignored in the history of the Valley is beekeeping. In researching this section, I was amazed at how much was written about the honeybee industry in nineteenth-century newspapers and agricultural magazines. It was called "bee ranching" and, once in awhile, "bee farming." Many of the early settlers were involved in beekeeping either on a full- or part-time basis or had a hive or two for their own personal use.

Honeybees are not native to the Americas; the German or European bees were introduced to North America in the early seventeenth century. There already were native bees, other nectar-loving insects and the wind here that did a quite adequate job of pollinating plants in the natural environment. However, the early European settlers planted artificial orchards with their concentrated needs for pollination and also brought their taste for honey. Some of the domesticated bees escaped and became wild or feral honeybees. Native Americans called the honeybees "white man's flies."

The earliest honey gatherers were nomadic people who would come upon a wild colony and obtain the honey by smashing the honeycomb, which destroyed the colony. In the Middle Ages, the very picturesque "bee skep" was used: a round, dome-shaped, coiled straw structure with a small hole to allow the bees to enter and build their brood and honeycomb. In order to extract the honey normally, the hive had to be destroyed and the honey strained, but the skep could be reused. The skep is experiencing a rebirth for decorative use or for nostalgia, but it cannot be used for commercial beekeeping due to disease-control issues. Using skeps is very inefficient, and many attempts were made to invent a better, more productive way to harvest honey.

It was not until 1850, when an English immigrant, Reverend Lorenzo L. Langstroth, published his book, *Langstroth's Hive and the Honey-bee: The Classic Beekeeper's Manual*, that the bee industry became highly productive. This book has never gone out of circulation and is widely used today. Langstroth is considered the father of modern beekeeping, as he invented the movable-comb beehive, a rectangular box with vertical frames that can be removed and let the honey be extracted without harming the wax comb, allowing the bees to refill the comb without having to start from scratch. The Langstroth hive is still the most widely used hive today and was the hive of choice for Southern California beekeepers. Modern beekeeping is not very different than from what occurred in the past; we have changed, but bees haven't.

Honey was one of the major industries in California in the nineteenth century. The first bees were brought to the city of Los Angeles by a prominent nurseryman, Ozro W. Childs, in March 1855. He bought hives of Italian bees in San Francisco for $100 and set them up in his nursery at

Twelfth and Main Streets. Growing bees in the city limits of Los Angeles did not last long; there were mainly only pepper trees for the bees to feed on, which made undesirable pepper-tasting honey. The bees agitated horses and swarmed around winery vats, disturbing the workers, and as the city became more populated, feral swarms disturbed the residents. By the 1880s, there was a $500 fine if caught raising bees witihn city limits.

The bee industry quickly spread to the foothills. The canyons of Southern California, and especially Los Angeles County, were considered to be the finest beekeeping area in the United States if not the world. The weather was ideal, as there was no bother with frosts, freezing weather or humidity; there was also a longer producing season, with plentiful mountain sage and native plants to feed on.

Beekeeping was considered a light industry, suitable for a full- or part-time basis and a good occupation for invalids and women. A full-time commercial beekeeper is called an apiarist. The apiarist not only raises bees for honey and beeswax but can also hire out his hives to pollinate orchards, sell established hives, raise queen bees for sale and remove feral swarms from residential areas where they are not desired.

A worker bee only lives four to six weeks, while a healthy queen lives three to four years, laying up to 1,000 eggs a day, or about 1 million in her lifetime. She leaves the hive only once, to mate with several drones. This one mating lasts her entire lifetime. European queens, especially the Italian variety, were the most desirable, as they are very docile. A wild colony can be contained and reestablished in a hive with a European queen bee and quickly transformed into a more manageable one; this is true even of today's aggressive African bees.

The hives were set up in the mouths of the canyons, where there was abundant wild sage and other native plants to feed on, away from domesticated animals and human traffic. The bee house would be located there. A bee house is basically a one-room structure used for extracting the honey and, when needed, sulfuring the hive to get rid of various pests.

Except in times of stress or drought, bees do not need to be fed or provided an artificial water source. With the frame hive, the vertical combs are removed, the top layer of wax is removed with a honey knife and then the comb is put into a honey extractor, which is spun around with a hand crank—the honey is released by centrifugal motion, causing the honey to fly out of the comb and run to the bottom of the extractor. The honey is drained through a spigot at the bottom of the extractor, filling sixty-pound tins with five gallons of honey. The honey is allowed to sit for twenty-four

California White Mountain sage covered the foothills and provided pollen for the bees.

hours; the hive debris floats to the top and is skimmed off. Two of the tins were packed into a crate for shipping back east or to Europe.

The yield per hive varies according to different reports, from 150 pounds to a whopping 500 pounds per hive in a season, with an average yield in good years of 200 pounds. Hives were regulated by permit, inspected and taxed; by 1886, there were estimated to be twenty thousand hives in Los Angeles County. In our modern day, due to decreased pasturage, hive yields average 75 pounds per season.

In the 1880 census, Valley residents Ford McClellan, John Harken, Frank Dunsmore, Edmund Weaver, Price Lewis, Theo Pickens, Henry Beckley, Felix Berry, Chester Williams, James Beamis and Nelson Van Tassel all listed their occupations as "apiarist." In the 1896 La Cañada Precinct Voter Registration records, William Bracken, John Joseph Johnson and Asa Rowley also listed their occupation as such. To have a commercially viable operation, they would have had at least one hundred hives.

Theodor Pickens, who is believed to be the first permanent white settler in the Valley, was a lifelong beekeeper. In his 1878 land patent application, he listed among his improvements to his land a bee house. In the 1800 census, he listed his occupation as apiarist, and when he died in 1923, his estate assets listed two hives and a honey extractor. Henry Beckley of Hall Beckley Canyon raised bees in Glendora, according to in the 1870 census. Charles Pate mentioned that he first met Frank Slutman in Glendora, where Frank had bees in Dalton Canyon, and that local storekeeper James A. Bone had bees in the canyon.

Dr. Benjamin B. Briggs, the founder of La Crescenta, came to the Valley in 1883 and was a very successful farmer; he grew many diverse crops, had a vineyard and kept bees, both for the cash crop and for pollinating his orchards. In a June 7, 1887 letter to his wife, Caroline, who was staying in Long Beach, he wrote about his honey crop:

> *I have been working with my bees, just finished the first extracting making a haul of about 300 lbs. and from this on for about 8 weeks. I must spend most of my time with them milking each hive about every 7 days and take from them their stores of the week. Many of them died during the long cold rain but those which came through are doing nicely now. So the next round I shall hope to get 600 or 700 lbs. but the extracting business though sweet is very hard work and could I hire some one to do it rightly I would be glad for I have so much else which ought to have my attention.*

Bears still roam the foothills and venture down into the residential canyons to scavenge for food.

The Bathey family also raised bees, as recounted by Herbert and Eudoxie Escalle Hall Bathey in a December 21, 1957 article in the *Los Angeles Times*: "Another interest shared by the Batheys is their bees. Both have worked with bees most of their lives and at one time Mrs. Bathey was one of the largest commercial bee operators in the La Crescenta area."

Making a living raising bees was a roller coaster ride, affected by frequent droughts and fires in the canyons, which destroyed the bees' sources of food. An August 15, 1904 article in the *Los Angeles Times* mentions the Valley:

> *BAD YEAR FOR HONEY MAKERS*
> *Worst Season Yet for Pasadena Bee Men*
> *Many Colonies in Danger of Starving to Death and Artificial Food Being Fed to the Bees in Many Places—La Canyada Ranchers More Fortunate.*
>
> *Through La Canada Valley there are bee farms that have succeeded. Mrs. Vellet* [Rosalie Veilex] *did well last year. Mrs. Simmons has always made a good thing of her bees. At the Turner* [Edson] *farm an interesting story is told of small beginnings. Four years ago starting with fifteen captured hives, there are now sixty hives after selling twenty-five. Edwards of La Canada always manages to bring his bees through the hardest season and it is taken for granted that he will do so this year.*

Beehives attract ants, skunks and 'possums, and bears were a constant problem as well. Tom M. Hall recounted a story about a bee incident to Grace Overbeck in 1938 for her book *A History of La Crescenta and La Cañada Valleys*:

> *Mr. Hall had taken a partner, but in those days there were no legal forms to be filled out and signed by the party of the first part and the part of the second part—a man's word was good in any business deal. When they divided the honey crop, it was just a case of putting a rock on the top and an "H" on the side of every other hive, and the partner's initials on the remaining ones. One day, they found the covers off every other hive that did not have the rock on top—and the honey gone! Finger printing was not popular then, but the thieves had left plenty of footprints—bears!*

TO VEIL OR NOT TO VEIL

Looking at pictures of modern beekeepers suited up, one could easily get them confused with someone working at a toxic waste plant. While it is recommended that one wear light-colored clothes around bees, it is highly unlikely that the early settlers wore elaborate bee suits, and early engravings and illustrations support this. With the introduction of the gentler Italian bee, many beekeepers worked without veils or gloves.

John Crane (nephew of La Crescenta founder Benjamin B. Briggs) at his apiary in Santa Barbara; he obviously did not feel the need to "veil," even though his wife did. *Courtesy of Lori Ward Kent.*

Even modern beekeepers do not like to work with gloves. Bee suit or not, if you work around bees, you are going to get stung—one usually acquires an immunity to the venom over time. The 1895 edition of *ABC of Bee Culture* noted:

> *Veils. The necessity of using face protections will depend very largely upon the race of bees to be handled. If you are to deal with hybrids, Cyprians, or Holy-Lands, I would recommend you to wear a veil. With pure Italians it is not so necessary, still I always prefer to have one handy.*
>
> *There are two great objections to the use of veils; one is that they necessarily obstruct the vision more or less, and the other is that they obstruct the free circulation of air, which is so desirable in hot weather, and thus tend to make the wearer sweaty, uncomfortable, and perhaps nervous.*

THE CHARACTER OF A BEEKEEPER

Bees are highly excitable, and the hives need to be approached from behind in a nonaggressive, gentle manner; bees can even become agitated from the vibrations from heavy footsteps. They communicate with their "bee dances" and chemical smells, and this makes them very sensitive to animal odors, especially bears and horses, as well as strong human odors. Even with a partner, beekeeping was a solitary profession. According to the article "Bees in Southern California" from the October 15, 1881 *Pacific Rural Press*:

> *The bee-keeper usually lives upon government land, not because he is unable to purchase what land he requires (which is a small amount), but because the wild sage, button sage, sumac and other honey flowers and shrubs are growing luxuriantly where land considered worthless for grazing or cultivation is left unclaimed and undisturbed. In almost every accessible*

Bill's Bees, a modern bee apiary in Angeles National Forest. *Courtesy of the author.*

> *gulch, gully and valley where water can be had—for bees use much water—and where the white sage blossoms, a bee ranch may be discovered. They are solitary places, veritable hermitages, where intruders from the outside world seldom find their way. Many of them are very beautiful little rural gems, set within a bower of roses and honeysuckles. These bee-raisers cultivate a sort of free-masonry among themselves, and aid and advise each other when called upon. They soon become accustomed to their solitude, and gradually accumulate a competence. There are a few exceptional cases where men have failed in bee-keeping, but they are few. No one should attempt to keep a bee ranch in this country unless he is a lover of solitude.*

The January 9, 1892 *Pacific Rural Press* noted:

> *Mr. W.M. Bomburger, in an essay read at the Iowa State Convention, states: "You never saw a lazy or stupid person succeed with bees. The successful bee keeper is an industrious person; a mechanic, a botanist, a good salesman and rarely a scamp. He gets all these truths from the hive. He can even get his religion from it."*

So what do we know about our early apiarists? They were solitary, knowledgable, industrious, could be gentle and nonaggressive and had relatively good personal hygiene.

CHAPTER 2

THE 1887 CRESCENTA HOTEL WINDSTORM DISASTER

Dr. Benjamin B. Briggs, the founder and developer of La Crescenta, offered special sale terms for anyone building a hotel in the Valley for tourists and invalids. Plans for a hotel seem to have started in 1885; he also promoted the establishment of a church, a town center and a schoolhouse. While there were sanitariums and boardinghouses already established, this was the first proper hotel with public dining service, elegant surroundings and meeting facilities.

The Crescenta Hotel was located on the northeast corner of Foothill Boulevard and Rosemont Avenue. The original hotel was built in the spring of 1887 by Los Angeles real estate dealers John Willey and S.B. Sanborn. It was built of wood and plaster on brick pillars, was two stories tall, contained twenty-four rooms and was completely furnished. In later years, the hotel site would be lushly landscaped with large trees, but in 1887, there were no trees to provide windbreaks. No known pictures survive of the original hotel. After the establishment of a local post office in 1888, "La" was added to "Crescenta" to differentiate the community from Crescenta City, California. Soon the hotel would be called the La Crescenta Hotel and, much later, the Silver Tree Inn.

Disaster struck in the early hours of December 14, 1887. High winds had been blowing in the foothills for three days and got increasingly worse. Some residents, fearing that their houses would blow down, took refuge in the new concrete schoolhouse. The hotel did not survive the winds and totally collapsed, causing injury and taking the lives of two people. The December

15, 1887 *Los Angeles Herald* and *Los Angeles Times* both had extensive articles on the tragedy. Some of the information and witness statements are contradictory, as is to be expected when they are quickly written to make newspaper deadlines. It was estimated that the winds were ninety miles per hour. The articles show the community spirit in the Valley, as residents, in spite of the high winds, immediately came to the aid of the survivors.

Two other buildings in the Valley were destroyed, one of them belonging to Sumner L. Spencer, a farmer, agricultural agent and occasional Valley correspondent to the *Los Angeles Times*. His first daughter was born in March 1886 in La Crescenta and was named Elsie Crescentia. Spencer was one of the residents who immediately got out of Dodge after the windstorm. In a January 8, 1888 testimonial letter in the *Los Angeles Times* for Dr. Sanders' Electric Belt, Spencer is noted living in Covina, and there is no evidence that he ever returned to the Valley.

Builder John Willey was the proprietor of the hotel and lived there with his wife, Delphena, and three daughters, Bertha, Anna and Daisy. He had recently hired Edwin G. Arnold, a forty-seven-year-old Civil War veteran, to manage the hotel. Edwin and his father both had experience as hotel managers. Arnold brought with him his wife, Clementina Murphy Arnold (forty-five) and daughters Claudia Mae (ten) and Edwina (three). Two older daughters, Nellie Inez and Jennie, were married and living in the Los Angeles area. Clementina and Claudia were killed in the hotel collapse. Edwin immediately went to Los Angeles to make funeral arrangements and to notify his daughters. He never remarried. At the end of his life, he lived in South Pasadena with daughter Jennie and her family and died sometime after 1913. Following are excerpts from the December 15, 1887 *Los Angeles Herald* article:

> *A Fearful Storm*
> *Terrible Accident in the Crescenta Canada.*
> *The Hotel Blows Down*
> *Two Persons Killed—Reports of Damage Done in the Outlying Towns*
>
> *One of the most destructive gales that has ever swept over Southern California is the one which started last Saturday night, and at the hour of writing is still continuing with unabated fury along the foothills of the Sierra Madre Mountains. Great destruction has been done to property all through the country and early yesterday the horrors culminated in a tragedy at Crescenta Canada, in which two lives were lost and fourteen persons lie suffering from the effect of their injuries.*

About eight months ago Messrs. Willey and Sanborn erected a twenty-four room hotel at Crescenta Canada, in the Canada Valley, twelve miles north of this city. It was built of wood and plaster after the style after houses usually erected in this southern country and was opened to the reception of visitors and as a boarding place for the residents of the district. Two weeks ago Edwin. M. Arnold undertook the management and with his family, consisting of a wife and two children, moved out there. Quite a thriving business was done, and when the present week opened it found the hotel accommodating a large number of guests, fifteen of whom were lodging there.

On Tuesday night most of thriving business was done, and when the present week opened it found the hotel the guests had retired to the rooms at the usual hour, but few of them could sleep, for the wind was howling without and the house creaked and swayed from the effects of the fierce currents of air which came sweeping down the valley. About midnight the situation became so serious that is was decided to abandon the building and seek shelter until daylight came, behind some mighty rock which would serve to ward off the onslaught of the wind. It was about 12:20 when Arnold said to his wife: "You have better dress yourself and the children, and we will leave the house," and going to the door he opened it and looked out into the midnight blackness without. The wind almost tore the door from its hinges, and hastily shutting it he stood inside, waiting for his wife to join him. Suddenly there was an awful crash, the lights were extinguished and he was struck to the ground by a beam of timber, which knocked him momentarily unconscious.

In the meantime the neighbors in the vicinity of the building had become aware of the calamity and hastened to the spot with lanterns. On arrival a strange sight met their gaze. A mass of timber piled confusedly upon the ground occupied the place of the hotel, and voices imploring assistance sounded form from amid the ruins.

A long account followed describing finding Mrs. Arnold near death, crushed by a timber and crying for her baby. She died in Edwin's arms. It was believed that the hotel would not have collapsed if Edwin had not opened the door. The next day, Coroner Meredith proceeded to the scene of the accident and held an official investigation, returning to Los Angeles at 6:00 p.m. He was seen by a *Herald* reporter, into whose hands he gave the following documents:

The jury decided that the deceased, Clementina S. Arnold, a female, married, a native of Pennsylvania, age about 45 years, came to her death on the 14th of December from injuries received by the falling upon her of a building known as the Crescenta Hotel building, at Crescenta, during an unusual windstorm, and the jury believe the said building to have been insufficiently braced and supported in its foundation.

A similar statement was made regarding the other victim, the personal description being "Claudia Arnold, a female, born in Minnesota, aged 10 years." Following are some of the witness statements from the coroner's report:

John Willey: "I reside in Crescenta. I am a real estate dealer by occupation. I am also proprietor of the Crescenta Hotel. I and S.B. Sanborn are owners of the building that is down. I never examined the building until after we had had a very heavy wind-storm last Saturday night. I then thought that the building was not braced sufficiently. I intended to get some timber to brace the building up, it was my intention to have it braced up as soon as I could. I did not think at the time that the building was in a dangerous condition. The building was built by contract."

John B. Cryer: "I reside in Crescenta; am a bricklayer and plasterer. Last night between the hours of 12 and 1 o'clock I was in the school house. I went there because the wind was blowing unusually hard, and I was afraid that my house was not safe. I was sleeping near a window in the school house. I looked out of the window and could not see the hotel, I got up and dressed and I went to work. I helped Mrs. Willey's little girl out of the wreck and several other persons. I then hunted for the other persons that were still missing and after cutting down into the wreck I found the bodies of the deceased. They were crushed to death by the building falling on them."

Ulysses E. Shaffer: "I am a hack driver by occupation. I have known the deceased about a week. About fifteen minutes after 12 o'clock last night I was in bed asleep. I woke up. The people in the house were up and walking around. The wind outside was blowing almost a gale. The building shook slightly just before the crash came. I was in bed. I was covered by pieces of the broken house. I could not get out. I called for help. We heard the persons on top of the debris cutting down to us, I was assisted out. I was hurt and taken down to the schoolhouse."

In conversation, Coroner Meredith said: "The gale is still blowing down there at a terrific rate. As I went up the hill to the town it was almost enough to blow the buggy over. The people in the vicinity have all abandoned their houses as they are fearful of further disaster, and are finding shelter and protection where best they may. Most of them are staying in the school house, which is quite a substantial building."

The *Los Angeles Times* article from December 15, 1887, recounts that some neighbors had sought safety in the hotel. The Arnold family occupied quarters in the back of the lower story. Around midnight, Edwin put out the kerosene oil lamps in the hallway and substituted candles, which were not as likely to cause a fire in case of a wreck if the building blew down. His wife and children were still in the back of the hotel:

CRUSHED TO DEATH
The Wind Gets in Its Deadly Work at Crescenta
Big Hotel Goes Down and Carries Death and Destruction with It
Mrs. Arnold and Her Child Meet with a Horrible Death.

He was in the act of doing this [securing the front door] *when there was a crash, and in an instant all was darkness, and he found himself lying in a little vacant space and imprisoned by broken timbers and loosened brick. Above the noise of the wind he heard the cries of others who were imprisoned by the wreck. In a few minutes Mr. Holly, who lives near the hotel, came with a lantern. Mr. Arnold called to him. After some work he was released and at once proceeded to the rescue of his family. He called to them that he was safe and was coming to their relief, but received no response except from his youngest child* [Edwina] *who kept crying out, "Where are you, papa?"*

The following were taken from the wrecked building, none seriously injured, but all more or less bruised; Miss Mary Merrill, Dr. G.W. Van Schaack and wife, Mrs. Durrell, Mrs. John Willey and three children of this city, Willie Wright, aged 10 years, a young man named Shaffer who drives the Crescenta stage, Mr. Arnold's youngest child, a girl aged 3 years. Mr. Berry, a consumptive from Kentucky was blown or fell out of the second-story window as the building went down, and was unhurt.

It is thought Mrs. Arnold was choked to death, as a piece of timber was found across her neck. She had been heard by those first at the wreck to cry out once or twice in smothered tones, "Where is my baby?"

The *Times* reporter made an odd observation: "Mr. Arnold came to the city yesterday morning, bringing his little girl. He is staying with his son-in-law, on Olive street, and is almost heart broken over his terrible loss." *Almost* heartbroken? What would it take, in the reporter's opinion, to be heartbroken?

Mrs. Arnold and Claudia Mae's bodies were taken to a neighbor's house, and in the morning, Edwin took them to Los Angeles, where his two married daughters, Nellie Inez Hale and Jennie A. Salisbury, lived. He never remarried and died sometime after 1913. A story has gone around that the Arnolds moved to California to get away from the Midwest tornados, but there was no mention of this in the newspaper articles or any other accounts of this that have been found. They most likely moved to California because Arnold's sister and two oldest daughters lived in Los Angeles.

HOUSES BUILT ON SAND

A very long, unsigned letter in the "Letters from the People" section was published in the *Los Angeles Times* on December 21, 1887. Here, in part, it blasts the construction of the hotel and gives a good description of the structure:

> *I personally know why the Crescenta Hotel went down before the wind. It went down because of its shape and its defective putting together. The hotel was long, narrow and high. Such proportions are well enough for the edifices that make up a city block, because, in a city block, the edifices support each other. Next, as to the putting together of the hotel. It was set on brick pillars, only two bricks to the course. In other words the pillars were about nine inches square. The pillars were from six to eight feet apart. The building was not sufficiently braced. The fall of the building surprised no one in Crescenta.*
>
> *The maximum pressure of the gale against the Crescenta Hotel hardly exceeded 10 tons. Properly constructed, it would have stood out against a maximum of three times that pressure.*

REBUILDING

The total loss was estimated at $10,000. The hotel would have assuredly been mortgaged and have had insurance. It was quickly rebuilt by Willey, more substantially, with thirty-two rooms. They were able to host a Thanksgiving dinner in November 1888. In 1964, Anna Caroline Crane, granddaughter of Dr. Benjamin B. Briggs's second wife, Caroline Amelia Crane Briggs, donated letters and poems written by Mrs. Briggs to the Huntington Library Archives. Most of Caroline's letters were written to her daughter, Sophia, and son, Benjamin, when they were living back east and she was living in La Crescenta. She also wrote a narrative about the first Thanksgiving dinner at the hotel, and it is published here with the permission of the Huntington Library Archives:

> *Thanksgiving Day 1888*
> *by Caroline Crane Briggs*
>
> *The hotel in La Crescenta situated in the lovely mountain valley north of us, set its first Thanksgiving table Thursday.*
>
> *About fifty persons set down in its well furnished dining room and feasted upon oyster soup, Turkey & Cranbery, Chicken Pie & Olives, Roast Pork, Celery with Green Peas & Lynash, Potatoes, Radishes & Lettis Miner & Pumpkin Pie, Cake, Apples, Grapes & Oranges—all the substantials of an old fashioned New England dinner with the luxuries of our Semi-tropical sunshine. The whole house was filled with the perfume of Roses & Helitrope & other flowers with which it was lavishly adorned. The rooms have a delightfully comfortable—the parlors are cheerful & pleasant & the halls—& airy…Many of the guests rode up from Glendale in Greys hack, returning after dinner, others—the larger part; spent the night, to see the sunrise on the Mountains, & the fog lie over the city. The merry games of the evening when all gathered into the parlor with the sweet voices blending in song made it the fitting ending of an ideal Thanksgiving Day & when those who tired in the town said Goodnight & went out into the starlight—they felt that the place must seem a restful home like retreat to the lone invalid seeking health among strange faces in our pure mountain air.*

There are many conflicting stories about the hotel and its various owners. Some say that it was built in 1890 by Mrs. Anna Fraley, burned down and was

A twentieth-century addition to the front courtyard of the hotel was the pond (with Olive Haviside Zimmer seen here) at the entrance to the Silver Tree Inn, one of the names the hotel was called over the years. The Zimmer family called it Stoneleigh. *Courtesy of Eugene Zimmer.*

quickly rebuilt; this is incorrect and unfortunately has been repeated many times. In actuality, the Fraleys purchased the hotel in December 1889, and there was never any fire. After the Fraleys bought the hotel, they continued the operations and, due to bad road conditions, delayed the grand reopening to February 22, 1890, Washington's Birthday. It was quite an affair, as described in excerpts from a February 27, 1890 *Los Angeles Herald* article:

> *Hotel Opening at La Crescenta*
>
> *Some time in December last the hotel of this place changed hands, the former proprietor, Mr. Durrell, retiring, and Mr. H.E. Fraley, of Las Vegas, assuming the management. The hotel was not closed, the changes being effected quietly. A goodly company gathered at the hotel in the mountains, a cordial welcome having been given to our neighbors to be present at a 1 o'clock dinner.*

The dining room was beautifully decorated, the word "welcome," in large letters of evergreen, greeting one upon entering; a long table, the entire length of the dining room, was laid ready, with epergnes of flowers and pyramids of oranges scattered at intervals along its length, The hanging lamps were decorated with trailing vines and flowers of nasturtiums; the walls were festooned with large branches of rose geranium and Monterey cypress, and the sideboard was decorated with flowers and huge branches of oranges. One of the party from Pasadena brought a camera; taking a photograph of the dining room before the party was seated. Eighty-eight guests sat down to dinner, the menu was as follows:

Clam Soup
Roast Turkey—Roast Beef—Roast Mutton—Cold Ham with Garnish
Tomatoes—Green Corn—Turnips—New Potatoes
Chow Chow
Horseradish—Pickles—Radishes, Lettuce, Crescenta Olives
Chicken Salad—Oyster Salad—Celery
Red Raspberry Jelly—Blackberry Jam—Preserved Ginger-root
White Cake—Fruit Cake—Rose Cake—New Breads
Plum Pudding with Wine Sauce
Currant Pie—Peach Pie—Cheese—Crescenta Oranges
Assorted Nuts—Raisins
Tea—Coffee—Wine

Tums, anyone? After the dinner was completed, the dining room was cleared for a dance, the music being provided by guests from La Cañada. The party did not disperse until midnight. Jacob and Ammoretta Lanterman were among the guests: "Nothing but praise was heard on all hands for host Fraley and his genial wife, who at present manages all the affairs de cuisine, employing only white help; 'no Chinese need apply.' Nearly all the prominent residents of La Crescenta were present. It was voted throughout a most successful affair and the popularity of the Crescenta hotel was well established."

The Fraleys only operated the hotel for four years, after which Hiram died. Some accounts have Hiram Fraley falling and dying of a broken back, but actually, he broke his leg and developed heart trouble. His wife continued to operate the hotel for several more years, as noted in this June 10, 1893 *Los Angeles Times* article:

LA CANADA

The Canadas have lost a valuable citizen by the death of Mr. Hiram E. Fraley, proprietor of La Crescenta Hotel, which occurred Tuesday morning. About two weeks ago Mr. Fraley fell from a wagon and broke his leg, but was recovering as well as could be expected, when heart trouble set in, resulting in his death in a few hours. Mr. Fraley removed from New Mexico to La Crescenta with his family about four years ago. He purchased and has since been proprietor of the hotel at this place. His untimely death was a shock to his many friends, and the deepest sympathy is felt by them for the bereaved family.

The following article, from the July 9, 1934 *Los Angeles Times*, gives a good idea of the significance of the hotel to the Valley:

GHOST HOTEL ECHOES GAY PAST
La Crescenta Building, Symbol of Old-Time Splendor and Rendezvous for Famous and Infamous Alike, Now Deserted and Decaying Structure

LA CRESCENTA. July 8—Is the La Crescenta Hotel destined to become a "ghost" building and stand as a shadow of the olden splendor that was once a mark of the gay life of La Crescenta Valley? This is a question old-timers are asking themselves.

The old building of thirty-two rooms, now vacant, was built fifty years ago. It has sheltered famous and infamous people, weathered severe storms, winds, rains and at last the recent flood. Its most recent episode concerned the Gettle kidnapping case.

A man by the name of Fraley, one of the owners, fell and suffered a broken back while unloading lumber on the grounds, and fate has dealt unkindly with others who have stayed beneath its roof.

Among the famous persons who made their home here while in the Southland were Ellen Beach Yaw, the California Lark. It was here she roamed through the hills, singing and learning the bird notes which startled Europe when she made her operatic debut in Paris.

Jan Paderewski, Polish pianist, stayed here, using the old rosewood square piano. Bob Wagner, publisher, and his close friend, Charlie Chaplin, sad-faced comedian, were guests. The late Thomas Leo Woolwine, District Attorney, stayed here during the last weeks of his life in the suite he had retained for years.

A hotel corner in the 1930s, now a large shopping center. Extensive landscaping covered the hotel grounds and hid the hotel from view.

St. Luke's of the Mountains can be seen across the street (Rosemont) from the driveway entrance to the hotel. *Courtesy of Eugene Zimmer.*

There is an old rubber tree standing guard at the foot of the front porch steps that is said to be very old, and ghost-like sounds at night are produced by the rattle of the tiny rubber balls dropping from the tree, while the litter of the leaves covers the porches.

La Crescenta Women's Club gave its first formal luncheon in the old dining-room, twelve years ago, with John Steven McGroarty as the speaker.

Louise Peet was once a guest and it is said that Clara Phillips hid away here, though that has not been proved. One suicide took place on the outside boundary of the grounds.

Lawrence Tibbett is said to have sung his way to fame in the old grape vineyard of the hotel.

It was at one time a boys' school. There Mr. and Mrs. N.O. Zimmer bought the place for their home and many happy parties were held.

The last chapter of the hotel's history was written when the kidnap cottage was used by the Gettle kidnapers was rented from Zimmer's real estate office, which stands on the south part of the grounds.

Today the grounds are littered with leaves, the rooms resound to the scurrying feet of mice and the flutter of bats' wings in the upper cupola rooms.

This article was rebutted on the same day in the *Los Angeles Times*:

La Crescenta Hotel Refuses to Be "Ghost"

La Crescenta. July 9. La Crescenta Hotel will not join the ranks of ghost buildings in California, according to plans of the owners, Mrs. G. Tetrick of Glendale announced today.

The famous old hotel will be remodeled and it is expected will once more take its place as one of the hostelries where people from all over the world will rest.

The plans include landscaping of the beautiful grounds which were once the mecca for visitors. Many of the fine old trees planted years ago stand in the spacious grounds.

The advent of automobiles brought smog to the Valley but also allowed people greater mobility to visit other attractions and more modern facilities. The hotel was torn down in the 1960s and replaced with a shopping center.

CHAPTER 3

A RAINMAKER COMES TO LA CRESCENTA

A quiet, unassuming Quaker, Charles Mallory Hatfield is the most famous rainmaker in the history of the United States. His controversial profession and life have led to many different views of his abilities, but he did manage to make a living out of it. Born in 1875 in Fort Scott, Kansas, his family moved to Los Angeles in the 1880s. Charles did not graduate from high school, but by the early 1900s, he had assumed the title of "Professor" and was known from then on as Professor Hatfield. He made an early living as a sewing machine repairman and salesman for New Hope Sewing Machine Company in Los Angeles, and by 1904, he had settled in Glendale with his younger brother, Paul.

"Rainmaker," "weather wizard," "pluviculturist," "cloud coaxer" and "weather modifier" were just some of names applied to rainmakers and the quasi-science of rainmaking at the time, but Hatfield preferred to be called a "moisture accelerator." While working in the sewing machine business, Hatfield read the 1871 book *The Science of Pluviculture* about crafting rain. He invented his own secret combination of twenty-three chemicals to induce thunder and rain. His rainmaking technique was to mix a secret batch of chemicals, climb up a tower and open the box of chemicals to disperse them into the atmosphere. He did not use a cannon or fireworks. An article from the 1970 *Journal of San Diego History* entitled "Hatfield: The Rainmaker" by Thomas W. Patterson gives what appears to be the most accurate account of Hatfield's early career:

Before he took his first paid engagement early in 1904, Charley built, with Paul's help, at least three other towers for experimentation. The first and most successful was near the mouth of Big Tujunga Canyon, November 6 through November 9, 1902. He said rains of three inches or more fell along the west–east line from La Crescenta through Pasadena, and 1.95 inches fell on downtown Los Angeles. Another higher tower was erected in Big Tujunga, near the present dam, and still another was at Inglewood, the Hatfield family home.

In 1904, the rainmaker's base of operation was neither at Pasadena nor Newhall. It was midway between the two at the foot of the present New York Avenue in La Crescenta. There in the brush contrary at the base of the mountains a tower some 20 feet high had been erected, surmounted by a platform 10 feet square. What appears in photographs to resemble a fume hood, somewhat narrower than those over stoves or laboratory cookers, protruded several feet upward from the platform. Beside it was a small pedestal surmounted by a narrow can—a rain gauge. At the base of the tower, Charley Hatfield and his young brother Paul camped in a tent.

Hatfield might have been seen, but for the isolation of the place, first helping to build the tower, then climbing up and down the ladder carrying loads. For hours at a time he might have been seen busy with something near the fume hood, out of the line of vision of anyone watching from the ground nearby.

He was 28, thin and of medium height. His hair was thinning slightly in front and receding at the corners. His face was narrow and the impression was sharpened by a long, thin nose. He wore a business suit as though he were in an office or ringing a doorbell in search of a sewing machine prospect. Paul, a boy of 17, was working equally hard—fetching, carrying, tending the camp and caring for the horses.

An elderly Englishman named Metcalf had a cabin a quarter mile away from which he tended a bee apiary. When he called at the tower to pay his respects and possibly to promote a conversation, Charley and Paul were too busy for more than a casual greeting. Later, after a walk, they returned to find Metcalf inside their tent. Charley promptly ordered him out. When Metcalf protested that his intentions were friendly and sociable, in keeping with Western custom, Paul leveled the shotgun and commanded, with all the authority a youth could must, "Get out of here!"

A week after they arrived, with the rain stopped, Charley and Paul dismantled the tower and stowed the lumber and some heavy trunks and the tent into their wagon. They drove southeasterly, following the dirt road that is now Honolulu Avenue, to Verdugo Road, then turned onto Colorado Avenue where they stopped at the little grocery operated by Joe Olivas. Charley bought a Times and for the first time saw himself discussed in a news story. Despite the doubting tone, it did report that Hatfield had gone forth and that rain had fallen.

Hatfield was quite secretive about his work, and it appears that Farmer Metcalf got his revenge for being so rudely treated, as he quickly went into Los Angeles and reported on Hatfield's experiment in La Crescenta. From the *Los Angeles Times*, dated August 2, 1904:

La Crescenta Farmer Tells Professor's Secrets
Derrick Was Too High or the Smell Was Too Strong or the Canyon Was Too Low or Something or Other Was the Trouble With the Machine.

"It never rains at all in Kansas.
When they want the rain to fall,
They shoot a cannon ball
And everywhere it rains—but in
Kansas."

Humming this classic ditty, Farmer Metcalf, he with the aching corns, followed Prof. Hatfield, the rainmaker, from La Crescenta, into town yesterday.

He was the only man who saw the rain-teaser at his mysterious work. The doings of J. Pluvius and the rain-maker in La Crescenta are supposed to be deathly secret, but Farmer Metcalf peeked and saw.

Gosh!

His is the only authentic account of the rain-teasing in the canons.

Rainmaker Hatfield is in town himself, having come to apologize for one of his rains having taken the bit in its teeth and killed a man forty miles away.

Farmer Metcalf says that the rain-maker began with a thin tall derrick. Under this derrick the rainmaker rigged up an extra strong barometer, double-toed and reinforced at the pants seat, made stout in readiness for the shock of the falling when the storm came whizzup.

Then, Prof. Hatfield peeled off to his undershirt and, taking a bucket of kerosene oil in one hand and tub of specially prepared dope in the other, started up the derrick, over a torturous succession of flimsy ladder rungs.

When he got to the top Prof. Hatfield scratched off a match and a wonderful smell went wafting off into the hills.

A turkey buzzard floating in high circles in the blue ether, ducked his head and flew for life. Down in the cañon, the rattlesnakes reared their noses on high and wriggled for cover. Kind-faced bumble bees, bumbling industriously over the mountain side, kicked up their heels and ran.

Prof. Hatfield gave a sniff of pleasant satisfaction and crawled back down the derrick for another pail.

Another and a wider odor smote the air. Prof. Hatfield was warming up.

Through the long forenoon they worked. Once his brother, whose job it was to stand at the bottom of the derrick and catch the falling barometer, protested.

"Say," he yelled up the derrick side, "It's awful hot down here."

A thin distant voice came down the derrick side. "Don't worry! It'll be real cool in the rain."

The sun went down blasting in a lovely blue cloudless sky. But the rain-maker was not discouraged. After dinner, when the night grew dark and buzzy with insects, the rainmaker shook out his pipe and gathered up his buckets again.

It was an evening shower he would have.

The black clouds soared skyward in thin wreaths of smell that made the mountain canons writhe in its sleep.

Suddenly from a distant mountain peak came a blinding flash. It was the searchlight from Mt. Lowe.

"Hurrah!" yelled the rainmaker, from his derrick top in triumph. "Hurrah! There's the lightning. In a minute you will hear the thunder."

The thunder, of course, did not come. That did not bother the optimistic rainmaker of the derrick top.

"That's all right," he said; "you'll hear it thunder all right before you go to bed."

But it turned out to be noiseless thunder.

Day after day for two weeks or more, the rainmaker besieged the clouds without avail.

But he was not disheartened.

News came that a man had been killed by lightning away off near Covina, and the rainmaker's face became downcast. He was filled with remorse.

At last, the day before he went home, one of the farmers strayed over and looked at the derrick in silence.

"Do you know what we have been doing?" the rainmaker asked impressively.

The farmer grinned.

"It was too high," added the rainmaker hastily. "Altitude too great."

"Too low in the cañon," suggested the farmer.

"Yes, that's it; too low," said the rainmaker.

"Guess the trouble is," said the farmer, "it's the wrong season for rainmakers. Guess you'd ought to wait until long about January in the rainy season."

Rainmaker Hatfield's great achievement, however, was in a dry spell. The credit of the rain he brought on then has been plagiarized by Dowie, Elijah II.

The fact is, however, that the prayers of Elijah II were hardly over before the downpour began.

Professor Hatfield started being paid for his rainmaking attempts, and although he settled permanently in Los Angeles, he traveled all over the United States and sometimes internationally, to varying success. It is said that the original play and 1956 movie *The Rainmaker* was based on Professor Hatfield and that he attended the premiere, but that was probably more of a press agent's promotion for the movie than anything else. The movie was about 1880s and 1890s flimflam men in the Midwest and was more of a love story than anything else. And the good professor certainly didn't look anything like Burt Lancaster.

Charles Mallory Hatfield died in Pearblossom, California, on November 17, 1965, and is buried at Forest Lawn Memorial Park in Glendale, California. He took his secret chemical formulas to his grave. La Crescenta's isolation was a perfect place for him to practice his early experiments and certainly provided a little excitement for Valley residents, especially Farmer Metcalf, he with the aching corns.

CHAPTER 4

Hunting in the Foothills

In the days before refrigeration, having a regular supply of fresh meat and poultry was not so easy. Local grocery stores only carried dry goods. After the Valley got more settled in the 1880s, peddlers would come up periodically from Los Angeles to sell meat, but most of the time, the people had to depend on themselves to put fresh game and fowl on the table. Deer hunting season was only six weeks, there were limits to the number of kills and it was kind of a feast-or-famine situation where everyone would have a lot of venison for a few days and then nothing. Rattlesnakes, wild fowl, jackrabbits, small game, home-raised chickens and eggs were other sources of protein.

Before the water in the foothills got managed, there were trout in the streams, sometimes artificially stocked, but after a forest fire in 1896 polluted the streams in Pickens Canyon, the fish never came back or were restocked. We can get an idea of what life was life back in the day from the words of the people themselves as recorded in Los Angeles newspapers—sometimes a bit exaggerated or flowery, but they still tell a story. Besides putting food on the table, hunting generated income via the sale of pelts, rattlesnake skins and rattles.

John Muir made a journey to Southern California in 1877. The following edited quotes are from John W. Robinson's book *The San Gabriels*, in which he described the rough conditions in the mountains:

> *The south front of the San Gabriels rises abruptly out of the San Gabriel and La Crescenta Valleys, culminating in pine- and spruce-clad summits*

John Muir in Eaton Canyon in 1877. *Courtesy of John W. Robinson.*

5,000 to 6,000 feet above sea leave. Steep, difficult of footing, coated with dense chaparral, this mountain rampart, to many an early Southern California settler, was a formidable barrier to travel and a natural boundary to settlement.

John Muir first sampled this mountain vastness in 1877. The great naturalist entered Eaton Canyon, then climbed a ridge to a high point near Mount Lowe, traversed the crest to the vicinity of Mount Wilson, and descended to the valley. He found the chaparral—rigid, thick, thorny—his biggest obstacle. "I was compelled to creep for miles on all fours," he wrote. He later described this south front of the San Gabriels as "more rigidly inaccessible than any other I ever attempted to penetrate."

RATTLESNAKES

If there was something plentiful in the Valley, it was rattlesnakes, the only venomous snake here. They were everywhere, and it was a daily occurrence in the early days to kill several rattlesnakes. The great majority of rattlesnake bites are on the hands, ankles or feet. Men wore boots or leather leggings to protect themselves. Generally, a woman's long skirt was protection enough for her legs. A healthy person will get very sick from a bite but will usually recover; the popular technique of cutting the wound and sucking out the poison, as generally depicted in movies, was not a common treatment. In the nineteenth century, getting blind drunk seemed to be the favored treatment, and there is some scientific evidence to support the effectiveness of this treatment. Contrary to depictions in movies, the snake must be coiled to strike and is only capable of striking about two-thirds of its body in distance. As a headline from the June 7, 1882 *Los Angeles Times* noted:

> *RATTLESNAKE BITES*
> *Cover the wound with baking powder, renewing every twenty minutes. A correspondent of the Yuma Sentinel is responsible for this. Probably his whiskey run low.*

Rattlesnake skins are easily peeled off and only need to be cured in salt. The flesh is considered very good eating, and it is reported that it tastes like suckling pig. The skins and rattles were very popular in the Victorian times, with an 1883 article in the *Los Angeles Daily News* reporting that the skins were used for belts, slippers, ties, bows and tassels. The rattles were incorporated into jewelry and highly desirable in mineralogy collections.

BRUINS IN THE FOOTHILLS

The bears in the San Gabriels were the now extinct (in the wild) California grizzly and the California black bear, which is pictured on our California state flag. Our current brown bears are not native to the area. Due to an overabundance of brown bears in Yosemite Valley, twenty bears were trucked to Southern California in November 1933, seven of which were released in the San Gabriels. There was a lot of controversy over this move, especially from the beekeepers, who said that the bears would destroy their hives. These bears are smaller than the grizzlies and black bears that once roamed the San Gabriels.

An odd article from the *Los Angeles Times*, dated May 15, 1883, noted the following:

Was It a Bear-Fight?
A Fierce Fight Between Monsters of the Sierra.

A correspondent sends us from La Canyada a description of a battle between big beasts of some uncertain sort, with the following note:

The sensations which the fight of monsters produced in me, the solitary auditor of the battle thunder of beasts, won't let me rest without affording others like, though second-hand, sensations.

Following is the way in which it occurred:

About 4 P.M. one of the days of last week, the mountains being invisible within dense clouds, a burst of mingled growls and yells resounded down a Sierra canyon that opens into La Canyada valley. The burst was not that of a battle of stallions for bulls, neither was it the harsh discord of huge summit boulders let loose and bursting down the mountain. Neither was it the jangle of a Yosemite leap of tons of iron bars. The angry burst was from animals as strongly-throated as stallions or bulls, and there was in it sound as solid as that of bursting boulders, and ringing as the jangle of iron bars.

Our informant approached the seat of war in the wake of the dogs. The dogs returned; full of the conviction that there was a battle, but over no bone of theirs. Our informant entertained corresponding convictions. Respectful distance, chaparral and trees precluded a sight of the belligerents.

Our informant does not undertake to say who the belligerents were. He, however, in a suggestory way, assists the conjecture of other by stating that there are huge grizzlies on the Sierras; that while they keep themselves most of the time on the north side of the mountains, the earlier grass, buds and tender, sugary flowerstalks of the yuccas on the south side—the side of the fight—naturally tempt the hungry grizzlies over. The flower-stalks of the yucca are not yet plentiful, even on the southern side of the mountain. The fight may have been between or among a couple or more bears about sugary yucca flower stalks in a place where the assemblage of bears outnumbered the yucca stalks, so that there was not yucca enough to go round.

This article deserves an award for the most words used to say absolutely nothing. The unnamed correspondent heard but did not see something in the bushes, and he made an entire article out of it. It must have been a slow day at the newspaper.

THE LAST GRIZZLY KILLED IN THE SAN GABRIELS

Cornelius Johnson originally settled in La Cañada as noted in the 1892 voter registration, but by 1900, he was a farmer and vineyardist in Tujunga. By 1916, things were getting relatively tame in the foothills, but a roaming bear was shot and killed in Tujunga by Johnson. There was a big barbecue for the whole town at Sunland Park, as reported in the *Los Angeles Times* on October 29, 1916:

> *Taste for Grapes and Honey Fatal.*
> *Huge Cinnamon Bear Killed at Sunland.*
>
> *A three hundred-pound cinnamon bear which had come to eat grapes in the local vineyards was shot and killed at Sunland yesterday morning a three-days' search by a hunting party headed by Cornelius Johnson. For about three weeks campers in the mountains back of Crescenta, Tujunga and Sunland have reported tracks of a large bear.*
>
> *When local vineyardists reported bear tracks the town people got busy, particularly after a valuable apiary was considerably damaged by Bruin's search for honey. Bear traps were ordered from Los Angeles, and the cynics smiled.*
>
> *Yesterday morning the local telephone wires announced the bear's capture and the whole countryside turned out. He had been trapped and had dragged the log to which the chain was fastened over a distance of a mile into the head of Fitzgerald Canyon.*
>
> *Sunland is going to have a barbecue of bear meat in the big county park today to celebrate the return of this stray visitor, which probably drifted around into the region from the Tehachapi Mountains.*

Johnson took the pelt to a Los Angeles hide dealer and found that he had actually killed a small, female grizzly bear, as reported in the *Los Angeles Times* on November 2, 1916:

> *Lost Coin by Killing Bear.*
> *It Was Silver-tip Grizzly and, Alive, Would Have Been Worth Large Sum.*
>
> *The bear shot at Sunland last Saturday, which was first announced as a cinnamon, turns out to be a fine specimen of a silver-top grizzly. Cornelius Johnson, who made the capture, brought the pelt down to Los Angeles and*

Cornelius Johnson and the last grizzly bear killed south of the Tehachapis. *Courtesy of John W. Robinson.*

> *learned, to his surprise and chagrin, that he had destroyed one of the most valuable specimens that have been found in California in many years. If taken alive, the bear would have been worth $1000. Had Mr. Johnson saved merely the bones for a skeleton, they would have paid him $250, but the bones and meat all disappeared at the barbecue. The pelt alone, however, is worth from $400 to $600, and in this Mr. Johnson feels some compensation.*

Museums valued the skeletons and pelts for their collections. This was the last known grizzly bear killed south of the Tehachapis.

A September 10, 1887 *Los Angeles Herald* article reports a hunting trip by Los Angeles residents to the Sierra Madre (San Gabriels) on the headwaters of the Tujunga River. What is odd is what they did with their booty:

Bear Blood Galore.
A Noble Band of Hunters March to Victory or Grief.

Bear steaks and venison will be hourly received at the Herald office, provided the burros connect with the train at Alpine or Fernando.

Why would meat be brought to a newspaper office? Were they selling it? How did they store it? Hopefully they had ice on hand.

ON THE WING

The following, from a May 1, 1885 *Los Angeles Times* article, is a good example of how nineteenth-century newspapers reported on obscure facts of people's lives:

The City

Will D. Beach shot a wild pea hen in the mountains back of Crescenta Cañada this week. These birds are said by the Mexicans to have been quite plentiful at one time. The specimen mentioned differs but little from the domestic pea hen. It is being prepared for exhibition by the taxidermist.

Peahens are the females of peafowl, which still populate parts of La Cañada, and the peacocks (the male peafowl) irritate current residents with their loud shrieking. They have been surviving here for a long time.

TURKEY SHOOTS: NOT EXACTLY A SPORTING CHANCE

There have been various mentions in Valley history about turkey shoots. These appear to have been an annual event usually done on Thanksgiving morning but sometimes on Christmas Day. The headline of a November 25, 1890 *Los Angeles Times* article noted:

A Turkey Massacre
The Arroyo Shoot Thanksgiving Day
A Big Bird for Ten Cents

The article starts by discussing a shooting contest for members of a Pasadena gun club before getting into the turkey shoot:

> *Following this will follow the turkey shoot proper, open for all, the only requirement being the payment of 10 cents for each shot fired. The head on a turkey will be arranged so as to just stick up above the ground. This will furnish the target at a distance of seventy yards from the marksman. One man may shoot until he hits the head at 10 cents a shot; then he gets the decapitated fowl.*
>
> *It will be the committee's aim to show everybody a good time. Free lemonade will be dispensed the thirsty assemblage and the comfort and entertainment of the visitors otherwise looked after. Visiting marksmen will also be present from other towns. The range is easily accessible from the foot of California street or by way of Colorado court and Sackville's Park.*

In other words, the turkeys didn't stand a chance! It is not known if the Valley men would hold their own separate shoot or joined in the with Pasadena shooters in the Arroyo. I wonder who was the lucky soul who got the privilege of cleaning and dressing the filthy, headless, bloody turkey for dinner.

PROTECTING YOUR TURF

The *Los Angeles Herald* reported on October 15, 1907:

Quail Are Now Ready
Open Season on Birds Begins This Morning
Feathered Dainties Reported in Large Numbers and from Every Direction, and Limit Bags Should Result

> *What would you do today if you were a quail? It wouldn't do any good sneaking off to the high hills or tall brush, for there will be enough hunters*

> *loose today to kill all the birdies in seven counties. The opening of the season will be about as big a thing as has happened in gundom in many months, and all kinds of things are in store for the quail.*

The article goes on to discuss the activities in various communities; this is what it reported about the Crescenta Valley:

> *Up toward La Canada and Crescenta the birds are unusually abundant, but the residents in that vicinity have decided to make a close corporation out of their district and fire all the outside hunters who venture into their territory. The low ground is well posted with signs forbidding trespassing, and the ranchers will be on watch for stray nimroads.*

The Deer Hunters

Deer hunting season was only six weeks, but I have to believe that if a stray deer happened to roam onto a ranch property, it would have been quietly killed. An extremely long article was submitted by an unnamed correspondent and gives a good description of the conditions that hunters encountered in the foothills. The correspondent appears to have been a gentlemen hunter from Pasadena and a member of the Alpine Club. Here are some excerpts from the December 5, 1886 *Los Angeles Herald*:

> *The Sierra Madres*
> *Deer Hunting in Their Fastnesses*
> *An Excellent Day's Sport*
> *What a Correspondent of an Exchange Says of the Mountain.*
> *Pasadena, October 29.*
>
> *Of all the mountains it has been my good fortune to enter, the Sierra Madres are the most deceptive and I might add attractive. From Pasadena that lies opposite the finest part of the range, they present a noble and impressive front. You are attracted to them immediately, so abruptly do they rise from the plain, and so symmetrical are their slopes.*
>
> *Months have been required to form a simple trail six or seven miles into the mountains and the rains of a single season often destroy the work*

GAME LAWS.

WHEN GAME CAN BE TAKEN

The deer season opened yesterday and several parties of hunters are now on the trail of game. Owing to a recent act of the Board of Supervisors of Los Angeles county it will be lawful to kill male deer until August 15.

In a recent ordinance it was made lawful to take game and fish in this county as follows:

Male deer, July 15 to August 15.

Quail or Bob White, December 15 to January 1.

Doves, August 1 to October 1.

Ducks, October 1 to March 1.

Black bass, July 1 to January 1.

Trout, April 1 to May 1.

Game laws for Ventura make it lawful to take game as follows:

Male deer, July 15 to September 1.

Quail or Bob White, October 1 to March 1.

Doves, July 15 to February 15.

Ducks, October 15 to March 1.

Trout, April 1 to December 1.

It is a misdemeanor in Los Angeles county to kill more than twenty-five ducks in one day.

It is a misdemeanor to shoot for sale or shipment quail, ducks, doves or other game protected by statute in Los Angeles county.

It is a misdemeanor to shoot for sale quail, grouse, ducks, doves, deer or mountain sheep, except from October 10 to October 15, in Ventura county.

Games laws in the nineteenth century were just as confusing as our present-day regulations.

of weeks. On the southern slopes, the mountains are not heavily timbered, but wherever the northern exposure is seen, there large pines and lofty trees appear, but elsewhere the manzanita, mountain mahogany, greasewood cover the slopes, forming a tangle almost impenetrable. The canons are like green rivers, reaching far down from the greater heights, and are the by-ways and lanes over which the black-tailed deer, the grizzly and other large game pass in their natural trips to the lowlands in search of the soft succulent grasses and other provender.

A hunting camp near Buckhorn in 1895. Note that there were women in the camp. *Courtesy of John W. Robinson.*

The party hired Eugene Giddings of Millard Canyon, nephew of famous abolitionist Josiah Giddings, to be its guide. Jean was a neighbor to Jason and Owen Brown. Many mountain dwellers, including the Browns, hired out to guide hunting parties. Local Valley residents would have known or gone with neighbors who knew the area and did not need to hire guides:

> *We were to follow the Giddings hounds in the morning, and an hour before daylight found us muffled in topcoats, our feet under the dogs that were piled into the great wagon, and whirling away up the great natural avenue of La Cañada, in the direction of the Hills. We followed the Cañada Valley several miles, then turned into the Verdugo. Our genial guide and master of the hounds dealt out the peaks of the range with lavish hand, and soon the would-be deer stalkers were ploughing through the greasewood making for the upper range.*
>
> *There are several ways of riding a horse up the side of a mountain covered with brush. When the angle is sharp one is to throw one's arms around the horse's neck and lay out lengthwise; another is to let the horse go ahead and cling to his tail. Both of these methods have their advantages,*

and I can recommend them and the horse stood the test. In the present instance, having a rifle across the saddle and the water canteens hanging from the pummel on either side, I merely put my trust in Providence and clung to a rope about the noble animal's neck, and with head on the horse's neck, we both butted through the scrub. I came out, as some one observed later on, "full of ticks and enthusiasm."

In the East the methods of shooting deer are often unsportsmanlike. But in the Sierra Madres the sport can be commended, as here the deer has all the advantage, and the sportsman must be a trained climber and a sure long distance shot, of the Giddings type, or no game is to be had. Nearly all the deer that he gets are killed across deep and wide canons, at a distance that in the East would not be attempted by a sportsman without a telescopic attachment.

The black-tailed deer, which is the common form here, is the Cariacus Columbianu. It is common throughout the entire State, often being found with the stocky and not particularly attractive mule. In some published works its flesh is described as poor eating. I find the reverse to be the fact. The black-tail is a purely mountain form, only rarely coming down into the valleys to feed, preferring the impenetrable mountain sides and the thick covers of manzanita and chaparral for its home.

Sam Hall's family was among the earliest settlers in La Cañada. Sam's first love was music, but he did share the Hall family passion for hunting. This article from the *Los Angeles Times* on August 14, 1902, gives a good picture of deer hunting in Tujunga Canyon, a favored spot of Valley hunters. The hunting season at that time was from July 15 to September 1:

GOT TWO DEER

Deer hunters declare that the quarry is pretty scarce this year. There seems to be about two hunters for every deer, with the hunters easier to locate than the venison. But deer are like gold. They are where you find them. Sam Hall of La Canada went out the other day with Gerald and Paul Waterhouse and they returned with two fine bucks that they got before they had been away from home two days. The game was flushed on a ridge of the Tujunga about twenty-two miles from the mouth of the canon.

"There are ways and ways of hunting doe," says Hall, who is a veteran mountaineer. "Most hunters make the mistake of starting very early in the morning and not finding any signs, they return disappointed at a time

Hunting party at the Hall ranch in La Cañada, circa mid-1890s. Theodor Pickens is third from left; Thomas S. Hall is on the right, sitting; Thomas McClellan Hall, his son, is to his right in the white shirt.

Skinning a deer at Barley Flats. Ranger Ben Reed (left) with hunter Rheinhold Guderian, a German immigrant who operated a grocery store in the valley in the late nineteenth century. *Courtesy of John W. Robinson.*

when the deer are most easily killed. Early in the morning the deer are out looking for food and drink, and they are very shy. They can hear the hunters scrambling about over the rocks and through the brush at a great distance, and they immediately get under steam for cover. They can travel a heap faster than the hunters. There's no danger of them being run down.

"On the ridges in the thick brush; you will see scores of burls scoped out by the animals. In these they lie during the warm part of the day. Take a good dog and you may flush them at close range. Even when roused from their rest, they only run a short distance before lying down again. So the time to get them is during the late hours of the morning."

There is a law in force which protects the does from being shot. The hunters laugh at this law, and defy the fellows who made it to distinguish a doe from a buck on the run. Deer won't wait long enough to have their sex identified. They are too busy. The fellows who made that law ought to catch the deer and label them with good big conspicuous labels, so that the hunters would make no mistakes. At this time of the year it is most difficult to tell a doe from a buck because the bucks are growing their annual horns. They lie out in the sun to harden them. You can't tell a doe from a buck nowadays by his horns because you can't get within a hundred yards of them. We shot seven or eight times at one of the deer we killed. They were both bucks, but it was only pure luck that we didn't kill does.

Newspapers of the day reported many incidents of hunting accidents, and deaths were blamed on amateur hunters who went up into the mountains for some adventure without being properly prepared.

COYOTE BOUNTIES

As civilization has encroached on nature, man and governments have tried to regulate the disruption caused by its presence. Laws and regulations abound over the management of wildlife. Complying with them is sometimes mind-boggling to a hunter, whether they are imposed by the federal, state, county or city governments. One extreme way to try to manage an out-of-control wildlife situation was to impose bounties. In 1891, a very controversial California state law was enacted offering a five-dollar bounty for coyote scalps. Coyotes were raiding farms and wreaking havoc on chicken ranches.

Hunters from Pasadena at Chilao in the Angeles National Forest in about 1900, when Chilao was far in the backcountry, two days' travel by foot or horse from civilization. *Courtesy of John W. Robinson.*

The coyote scalp had to include both eyes and ears and be not more than three months old. The local scalps were brought to the county clerk's office in Los Angeles, and the bounty hunter received a certificate for redemption. The clerk stored the scalps in the office safes or wherever they could find room. Each quarter, an accounting was sent to Sacramento requesting reimbursement. Once the county received the money, the hunters could redeem their certificates, and the scalps were burned. It could not have been an especially pleasant situation, storing a bunch of uncured scalps in the office, especially in the summer.

Five dollars was a lot of money in those days, and the program was immediately overrun with fraud. Scalps were being bootlegged from Mexico, and a large shipment from the Midwest was intercepted in Northern California. The program was so successful, though, that the state legislature was alarmed at the cost, and it remained a problem for the next decade. In the nine months ending on December 31, 1891, Los Angeles County received $6,005 in reimbursement, which represented 1,201 scalps. As is to be expected, when a predator is eliminated, other species are thrown out of balance. In less than a year, a jackrabbit bounty was enacted.

CHAPTER 5
WINE, VINES AND RAISINS

One of the major agricultural crops in the Valley was grapes. They were used as table grapes and raisins and also used to make wine, brandy, port, vinegars and many other byproducts. The Valley's climate and soil, as well as the fact that grapevines can be mostly dry-farmed, without major irrigation, made it an ideal crop for the Valley. A newly planted vineyard can start commercially producing within four years.

Even though some La Crescenta wines won awards at the California State Fair, the wine produced by Valley grapes was not estate quality, and many times, it was used for blended wines that were, for the most part, meant for immediate consumption. The variety of grapevines planted varied greatly. Some early Valley residents who planted vineyards were Dr. B.B. Briggs and George Le Mesnager in La Crescenta and Thomas S. Hall and Jacob Lanterman in La Cañada. Cornishon Avenue in La Cañada is named for the Cornishon grapes raised by the Petrotta family.

The original grapevines in California were planted by the Spanish missionaries in the late eighteenth century from a variety called Lesthan Prieto and were called "mission grapes." The name came from it being the only grape variety planted at the missions. It was very versatile, producing red and white wine, dry wine, brandy and a fortified sweet wine called Angelica, and it was also very good as a raisin grape. Its use has greatly diminished in the current growing era, but Angelica is still being produced as a popular dessert wine. The wines made from mission grapes were also referred to as "Old California" wines. Until 1850, the mission grape was the only grape grown in California; early French winemakers in the city of Los Angeles imported grape cuttings from France, and new varieties contributed to the decline in the popularity of the mission grape.

While we picture vineyards with upright, staked vines, this style of grape cultivation did not come into being in California until the late nineteenth century. Vines were not staked. They grew like bushes and were cut back to the roots after harvesting, and in the summer, the vines sprawled on the ground in a matted mass of low trailing vines—under their broad leaves, the grapes were sheltered from the heat of the summer sun. They were not netted; this method of growing grapes was less labor-intensive than our current system that produces higher yields.

RISE OF THE WINE INDUSTRY

In 1883, the California state legislature raised the tariff on imported wine, making the tariff alone more costly than buying local wine. This spurred the growth of the local wine industry, as noted in this November 23, 1883 *Los Angeles Herald* article:

> *The New Tariff*
>
> *In the last session of the Forty-Seventh Congress, the Tariff Bill is especially beneficial to this State and to the county of Los Angeles.*
>
> *The new law increases the duty of still wines from 40 to 50 cents per gallon, with no allowance as formerly for leakage. This tax will pretty effectually stop the importation of these wines into the State. They are rapidly disappearing as appears by the statistics of the Custom House. In 1872 the United States imported 5,972,423 galls of wine from France in the wood, while in 1881 only one third that amount was import.*
>
> *At the same time, the importations of wine from Germany declined from 988,450 gallons to 228,931. The tariff on these wines is now more than the wine are actually worth, and will drive this low grade of light wine from the State.*
>
> *Any person of intelligence can at once perceive that with a tax of fifty cents per gallon on light wines in wood, it will be impossible to import them because the California Zinfandel can be purchased for forty cents per gallon,*

while the foreign of similar quality will cost seventy cents without any profit to the importer.

GEORGE LE MESNAGER AND FAMILY

Although not a Valley resident, George Le Mesnager, a French immigrant, was a major wine producer in Los Angeles County. He had several vineyards in the Sparr Heights in Glendale and what is now Deukmejian Wilderness Park. He bought, along with his partner Pierre Durancette, what was then La Crescenta property from Dr. Benjamin B. Briggs in February 1886 that included the water rights in Dunsmore and Cook Canyons. Vineyards were planted, and the grapes were sent to the Le Mesnager Old Hermitage Winery in Los Angeles for processing and sale of "Old California" wine, brandy and port.

George stated that his vineyard was dry-farmed—that is, without regular watering of the vines. However, there was a water tank, and an old piping system was discovered after the 2009 Station Fire, so there was occasional watering of the vineyards, especially in drought years.

An article in the "La Crescenta" section of the *Pasadena Star News*, dated September 23, 1889, mentioned George Le Mesnager:

GRAPE GROWING

Mr. Mesnager, the wine dealer of Los Angeles, has a large vineyard in the Dunsmoor Canyon just above our valley, where he raises grapes for his use.

Old Hermitage letterhead.

The Stone Barn, located in Deukmejian Wilderness Park in Glendale, California.

> *He has been having a place cleared preparatory to planting a large vineyard south of here, and this side of Verdugo Park. It is said that the grapes raised in the mountains make a particularly delicious flavored wine, which it is important to obtain from grapes raised on low ground or difficult soil. It is here dryer and they obtain a sweetness and flavor, the effect of which desired by wine connoisseurs.*

In 1900, George's son, Louis, took over the winery operations, including the Dunsmore property. In the early 1900s, he built the large Stone Barn to house the equipment and grapes before transporting to Los Angeles. The 1933 fire in the Valley burned part of the Stone Barn, and it was rebuilt with a second-floor mezzanine as a residence for Louis's family. They lived there until the 1960s.

George gave an interview to the *Los Angeles Herald* for June 6, 1889, about marketing wine:

> *Yesterday, a Herald reporter held a conversation of half an hour with Geo. L. Mesnager, a well-known vine-grower of this city. In the course of this talk Mr. Mesnager said:*

We are making satisfactory progress with the business of making wines. We have still a good deal to learn. So have the consumers of wine.

Yes, we make an excellent port wine, it is as good as any made in any part of Europe. Now you see there are only certain districts in Europe where, after centuries of experience, they try to make port.

No, we do not make good sherry. Ah! You see there is only one little spot in all Europe where they make really good sherry. We have found the Los Angeles and San Bernardino grapes make the best ports; in fact they are the only port districts in the State.

Of course there is a good deal in the way grapes are handled. It will not pay to take the pains they take in Europe. I will take as much trouble in the making of my wines as they do in France when the market will warrant it. At present it will not. When I can get $2.00 a gallon for perfect wines, I will hand-pick each grape. Lafitte sells in France at $2.00 a bottle, and labor is cheap there. So is money. It costs something in interest for us to carry a vintage four years.

But we must not think we can make good port, good Burgundies, good Rhine wines and good sherry all on the same patch of land. Our vineyards where we make our clarets are high up the sides of the mountains, they are covered with snow every winter. They are 2,500

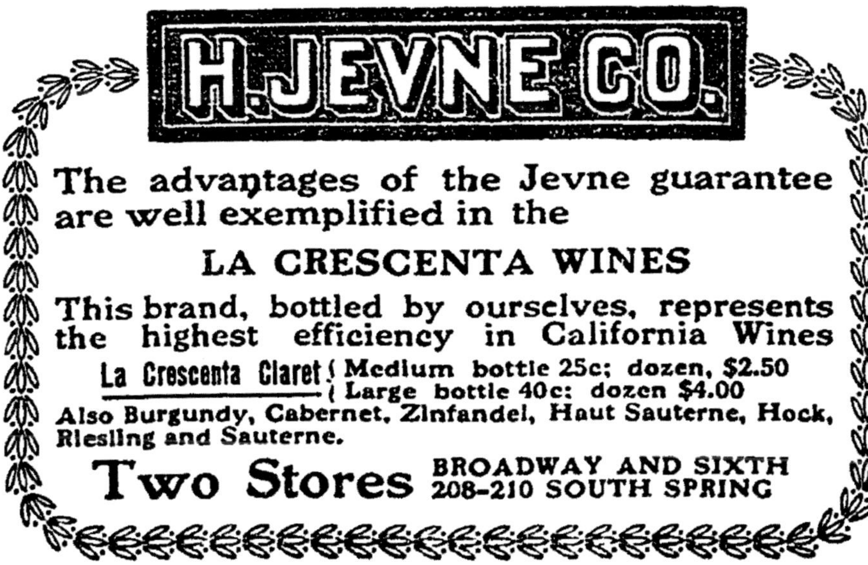

Hans Jevne was the exclusive bottler and seller of La Crescenta wines, olives and olive oil.

feet or more above the sea level. They are on steep slopes where it is hard to plow.

So you see we are learning. In time we shall make other sorts of wine at successfully as we are making ports, as successfully as I am making my Rousillion red wines. But the consumers will also have to learn to buy wines on their merits and not on their labels. They will also have to learn that there are different grades, and that they will have to pay more for wines carefully made, intelligently treated and kept until they mature, than they pay for the stuff called wine which is so often made without care, and sold as soon as the first fermentation is over.

HANS JEVNE, LOS ANGELES GROCER

Hans Jevne, a Norwegian immigrant, came to Los Angeles in 1882 and established an upscale grocery on Spring Street. He became the exclusive bottler and distributor for La Crescenta wines. He advertised extensively in the *Los Angeles Herald*, and his ads give a good picture of tastes and prices in the nineteenth century. He exclusively sold La Crescenta olives, olive oil and several varieties of wine. He also handled the bottling and packaging of the wine and olives. Some of the varieties of wine that Jevne sold included claret, Burgundy, Cabernet, Zinfandel, Haut Sauterne, Hock (a German-style wine), Riesling and Sauterne.

POLITICALLY CORRECT

Drinking wine, as opposed to hard liquor, was a much more socially acceptable option in the nineteenth century, especially for women. Even today, most of us have known someone who drank too much but didn't think it was a real problem as they only drank beer and/or wine. Before the Pure Food and Drug Act was established in 1906, there were no regulations on ingredients or claims to the efficiency of tonics and tinctures. A prominent advertiser in the *Los Angeles Herald* was Gilmore's Aromatic Wine, promising cures from everything from malaria to female "problems" and impotence in both men and women. A retail druggist and chemist, H.D. Godfrey, extensively advertised Gilmore's Aromatic Wine. Following are some of the testimonials found in the *Los Angeles Herald* in 1886 and 1887:

- Dr. Freeland, of the M.E. Church, says that two bottles of Gilmore's Aromatic Wine cured his wife of Nervous Debility and Sleeplessness.
- Rev. E.J. Whitney, says Gilmore's Aromatic Wine for Female weakness, stands without a rival.
- Impotency in man or woman cured by Gilmore's Aromatic Wine.
- Why Will You Suffer from Ague and Malaria when Gilmore's Aromatic Wine will cure you.
- Nerve-Life and Vigor restored in man and women by using Gilmore's Aromatic Wine.
- The Wife, Mother and Maid who suffer from female weakness, will find Gilmore's Aromatic Wine for female weakness, stands without a rival.

TROUBLE IN PARADISE

Some Valley farmers made wine on their ranches and sold wine by the jug. They needed a business license to do this and not everyone followed the rules, according to the June 20, 1906 *Los Angeles Herald*:

> *CHARGED WITH SELLING LIQUOR TO INDIANS*
> *La Canada Man Arrested by County Official*
> *Complaint Made that Rancher Made Wine Without License and Disposed of Product to Natives—Pasadena Officers Take Action*
>
> *Complaint was made yesterday morning against Joseph Deitl of La Canada for alleged illegal selling of liquor without a license, and late last night the man was taken to Pasadena by Constable Austin. Deitl will be given a preliminary examination today in the justice court at Pasadena.*

> *It is alleged that for the past three years Mr. Deitl has been making wine without a license at his place in La Canada. The customers of Mr. Deitl have been, it is said, Mexicans and Indians, and is alleged by the people of La Canada much disturbance has been made on account of drunkenness.*
>
> *Two years ago complaint was made to the district attorney's office that Deitl had been selling liquor to Indians, but evidence was not secured which would warrant the man's conviction.*
>
> *During the last three weeks a representative of the Pasadena police force is said to have secured abundance of evidence which with incriminate Mr. Deitl. The people of La Canada are said to be ready with facts which will show that wine has been sold to two Indians, and this fact is said to incriminate Deitl for selling liquor to Indians contrary to the federal law.*

On January 1, 1907, Manuel G. Verdugo, son of Teodoro and Maria Verdugo, was granted the first liquor license to conduct a saloon in La Cañada, over the objections of the residents of nearby Glendale.

RAISIN INDUSTRY

While raisin growing is still a major industry, its importance before the widespread use of refrigeration cannot be stressed enough. Raisins, as well as other dried fruits, were nutritious, easily transported and cheaper than canned goods. They kept people's diets varied, especially throughout the winter. Drying greatly extended the market for California fruit. Some grape varieties—such as mission, Sultana and Muscat—were preferred for making raisins; however, any grape variety can be used.

FRUIT DRYING

Many of the Valley crops were dried, and the procedures were basically the same for different crops. For raisins, the farmer either dried the grapes on trays in full sun or transported them to Los Angeles to a drying factory.

In 1874, the Alden Fruit Drying Factory was established, according to a *Los Angeles Herald* article from October 24 of that year:

> *The Alden Fruit Drying Factory just completed in this city by Mr. Geo. B, Davis, turned out its first raisins yesterday. They were manufactured from the Mission grape and confirm our prediction of some weeks ago that the Los Angeles Mission grape would turn out a raisin greatly superior to that manufactured from the same quality of grape grown in vineyards of Santa Clara, Alameda, Solano and Sonoma counties. The raisin from the Mission grape of those sections is now in the San Francisco market, and is in great demand for common use. It is small and wanting in saccharine matter. The raisin produced from the Mission grape at Mr. Davis' factory is nearly or quite double the size of that above described, and much sweeter and finer flavor. Several of our leading grocery firms, after a careful examination of the Los Angeles Mission grape raisin, pronounce it equal to the best imported Malaga.*
>
> *There is no longer any doubt but that the grapes of this valley will make a raisin vastly superior to that produced from the grapes grown further north.*

Alden also sold fruit drying supplies and patented a device called the Evaporator, a complicated drying rack that relied on heat and sped up the drying process. In 1881, the Southern California Packing Company was established and took over the original Alden factory located on the eastside of the Los Angeles River.

An 1885 newspaper article noted that drying depends on the weather—it is better to dry in the vineyard on trays and then send to packinghouses for final processing, shipment and grading. A hard rain could ruin a drying crop. Under the right conditions, it took about fifteen days to turn grapes into raisins. The raisins were packed in sawdust for transport. There was an old saying: "You put out your raisins for drying and prayed for no rain."

Many farmers preferred drying on site, as transferring fresh fruit to a drying facility required premature picking of fruit; at the farm, they could pick and immediately dry it when it was at its peak of ripeness and flavor. A June 30, 1894 article in the *Pacific Rural Press* recounted an interview with Theodor Pickens and his method of drying lemons:

> *Mr. Theodore Pickens, of La Canyada, suggests a plan for curing lemons, which he says he has tried successfully and which he calls*

> *"the poor man's method." He cuts his lemons from the trees, using all the ordinary precautions in handling, put them in regular fruit boxes, having openings at each end for the purpose of handling same. He then places his boxes on the north side of the house or in some shady place where the sun will not reach them, and packs five or six boxes high, putting a sack over the top of each and letting the ends come down over the openings at the end so as to exclude the air and light, About once a week he gives the lemons a shower bath of cold water by inserting the end of a hose in the openings at end of boxes. He repeats this operation about once a week, or, if the weather is cloudy, not so often. He produced some really fine specimens cured in this way, and he says he has kept them six or eight months. His Pearmain apples are kept by this method.*

Some crops, especially stone fruit such as apricots and peaches, needed to be sulfured and hand-pitted. The mechanical pitting devices of the day did not work very well and needed unripe, hard fruit to avoid being squashed; the devices were not popular. T. Fenton Knight was the son of Jesse and Elizabeth Knight; the family moved to California from Missouri in the late 1880s and settled on property in La Cañada. In 1954, T. Fenton wrote a column for the *La Cañada Valley Sun* titled "Early Recollections of La Canada." In one column, he described the harvesting and drying of the family apricot crop:

> *Early in July, 1887, the La Canada sun began to paint the green apricot trees in our orchard with blobs of golden yellow, and the harvest time for that crop was on almost overnight. The gang of four Chinamen who were housed in the oak grove camp did the picking. Joe Oldfield, the "hired man" hauled the fruit to the cutting sheds set up in the shade of several spreading oak trees, and the neighborhood women came in to pit and spread the seeded halves on the drying trays. These trays, after being stacked and thoroughly fumigated with sulphur fumes under an air-tight tent, were spread out on the ground to dry in the sun.*
>
> *The cutters were paid 5 cents per box for their work. The average cutter could pit and spread about 12 boxes per day, but we never had any shortage of help for the job afforded the women in the neighborhood the opportunity to make a little extra cash (a very scarce article in those days) and catch up on valley gossip at the same time.*

There is power in numbers, and farmers' cooperatives were formed to assist growers in transporting, whole selling, advertising and whatever was necessary to be profitable. The California State Raisin Growers Association was organized in 1883, the California Dried Fruit Association in 1888, the La Cañada Fruit Growers Association in 1892, the Grape Growers & Winemakers Association in Los Angeles in 1886, the California Cured Fruit Association in 1900 and the State Fruit Exchange in 1893. These cooperatives helped keep the market stable and avoid severe fluctuations in crop prices.

THE WINE TRADITION CONTINUES

Remnants of the early vineyards exist in the Valley on hillsides and in the backyards of homeowners, some of whom have no idea of their history.

A private vineyard, Beinn Bhreagh Vineyard, is located at 2,700 feet elevation in the foothills of La Crescenta. It is the highest-altitude vineyard in Los Angeles County. Planted exclusively with Pinot noir wine, the 2013

Beinn Bhreagh Vineyard, a modern vineyard in the foothills of La Crescenta. *Courtesy of Timothy Mac Donald.*

harvest is expected to produce seventy-five gallons of wine, well under the "home-brew" maximum of two hundred gallons, but will yield 360 bottles of wine.

A vineyard was reestablished by the City of Glendale at the Deukmejian Wilderness Park in 2004. It is located at the back of the historic Stone Barn built by the Le Mesnager family. The vineyard has eighty-one grapevines with three varieties: Early Burgundy, a pale, pinkish-red wine grape and a version of the French grape Abouiou; Allicante Bouschet, a cross varietal of the French grape Aramon and the Spanish garnacha grape; and Red Flame, a table grape.

After the 2009 Station Fire, some old vines were found in the hills above the Stone Barn still holding on. There are plans to expand the vineyard with several more rows of vintage varietals. A volunteer group, the Stone Barn Vineyard Conservancy, maintains the vineyard and harvests and bottles a small batch of wine in the fall.

CHAPTER 6

TURNER RANCH AND THE BEGINNING OF FLINTRIDGE

The history of Flintridge has many references to the Turner Ranch and its purchase by Senator Frank Flint, but beyond the mention of Turner, there is little information about him. Before finding this unknown Turner, we need to go back to the earliest days to see out how the property eventually developed into the community of Flintridge.

THE SPANISH PERIOD

When there were only native people living in what is now California, no one owned the land. Native people did not have a concept of land ownership, and their way of life was changed forever by the arrival of the Spanish in 1769. The San Gabriel Mission was established in 1771, and virtually all the local native people were moved to the missions or adjacent properties to be converted and to toil as workers for the padres in their extensive vineyards and cattle and sheep raising operations.

During the Spanish period (1769–1821), the ranchos were concessions from the Spanish Crown, permitting settlement and granting grazing rights on specific lands located outside missions, presidios and pueblo boundaries. The Crown retained ownership of the land.

In 1784, Rancho San Rafael, a 36,403-acre Spanish land grant, was given to Corporal Jose Maria Verdugo, a Spanish soldier who had served with the

1769 Portolà-Serra Expedition. The boundaries were primarily defined by the Verdugo Mountains, Arroyo Seco and the Los Angeles River.

MEXICAN LAND GRANTS

Mexico won its independence from Spain in 1821, and in 1834, the Secularization Act was established, with the Mexican government repossessing most of the lands held by the Spanish Crown. The missions were secularized, and the lands were awarded in Mexican land grants, forming many new ranchos. The Mexican land grants gave individuals ownership but had a few provisional conditions: the boundaries had to be officially surveyed and marked, and the grantee could not subdivide or rent out the land. The land had to be used and cultivated, with cattle and horses raised, and a residential house had to be built within a year. Public roads crossing through the property could not be closed. If these conditions were not met, the land grant could be challenged by another party who could then claim the land. This led to may disputes over rancho ownership in the ensuing years.

Rancho San Pasqual was formed in 1834 out of San Gabriel Mission land; it borders just to the west of the Arroyo Seco and formed the basis of the present-day cities of Pasadena, South Pasadena, portions of San Marino and Altadena.

Rancho La Cañada was established in 1843 out of the northern part of Rancho San Rafael. It was a large Mexican land grant given to a Mexican schoolteacher from Los Angeles, Ygnacio Coronel. He called the property *La Cañada Atras de Rancho Los Verdugos* ("Canyon behind the Verdugo Ranch"). The original Rancho La Cañada grant was about 12,000 acres. Jose Maria Verdugo's descendant, Julio Verdugo, disputed the grant, claiming that it was still part of his Rancho San Rafael and at some point regained some of the property, but not all was returned and/or sold off; 5,745 acres remained the property of Ygnacio Coronel.

After California became a territory of the United States in 1848, the Treaty of Guadalupe Hidalgo stated that Mexican land grants would be honored if the title could be confirmed. This was easier said than done and led to many lawsuits. In the case of Rancho San Rafael, the Great Partition of 1871 was enacted, dividing the rancho into thirty-one sections

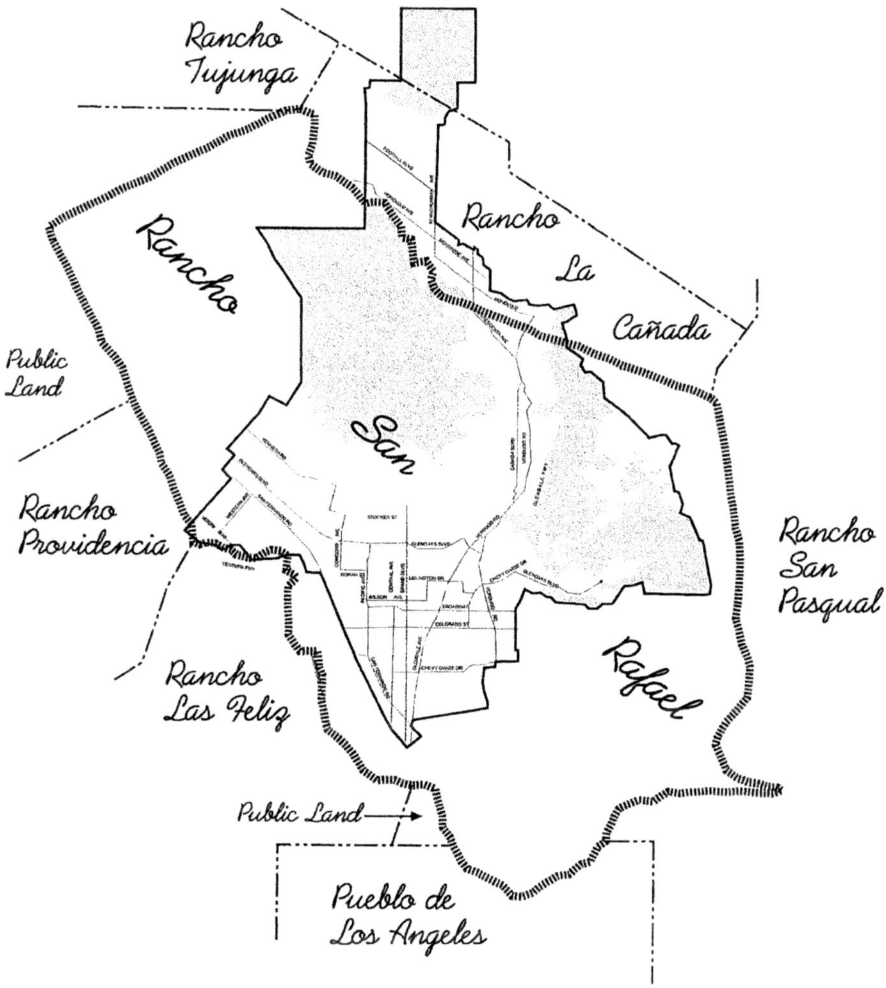

Map of the foothill ranchos. *Courtesy of Glendale Public Library Special Collections.*

among twenty-eight people, including a portion to the Verdugos. A German immigrant, Anaheim vineyardist Benjamin Dreyfus, was awarded an 8,424-acre portion south of Rancho Cañada; with Rancho San Pasqual bordering on the east, it extended south to what is now Eagle Rock.

The Spanish and Mexican land grant boundaries became the basis for California's land survey system and are still used in modern maps and land titles, as well as are shown in *Thomas Guides*.

WATT'S SUBDIVISION

Dreyfus owned extensive vineyards but did not develop his rancho property; he sold his interest in Rancho San Rafael in April 1883 to a partnership of Pasadena businessmen, according to the April 8, 1883 *Los Angeles Herald*: "The sale of B. Dreyfus' interest in the rancho San Rafael to Messrs. [Charles] H. Watts, M.L. Wicks, E.T. Wright and M.E. Hodgkins for $50,000, for the purpose of establishing a colony."

The description of the property as noted in the deed runs a page and a half on legal-size paper. The property was undeveloped, and there were no roads to mark boundaries. Points of reference include a large rock, stakes and a large sycamore at the southeast-side ditch.

They named the development Watt's Subdivision. An original map of it is located at the county recorder's office in Norwalk, in Miscellaneous Records Book 5 (maps 1 and 2). The June 1883 subdivision map was surveyed by E.T. Wright, one of the subdivision purchasers. It consisted of ninety-five lots of varying sizes, and the partners quickly recouped their investment, as reported in the *Los Angeles Herald* on May 11, 1883:

> *The new syndicate which recently purchased 8425 acres of the Ben Dreyfus tract for subdivision will at once commence the development of the splendid cienega in the Verdugo canon, and which has been "live" ever since Los Angeles was first founded. Experts in water development consider it certain that this supply can be quadrupled by property manipulation. This water, to be brought out in pipes, will be sufficient to amply irrigate the 2425 acres of rich land below the water level. As is well known, Messrs. C.H. Watts, M.L. Wicks, E.T. Wright and M.E. Hodgkins, were the incorporators of this grand scheme, having bought the Dreyfus tract of 8425 acres some time since for the sum of $50,000. Six thousand acres of this are rather precipitous rolling land, while the remainder is a plain of great richness, just inclining to the south enough to be irrigated easily and cheaply. The 6000 acres are as yet undivided, but the remaining 2425 acres are entirely cut up into small tracts. Sixty-three thousand dollars' worth of property has already been disposed of, with $30,000 additional now being sold, making a cash profit of $43,000 in a few weeks, and but 1,000 acres of the rough land disposed of, leaving 5,000. acres of that character on hand. Business energy, knowledge of land and water, have made this enterprise*

a grand and conspicuous success in a short time. The expense for water development, surveying, pipe laying, etc., has been about $10,000.

This is one of the most successful, bona fide, and excellently managed real estate ventures that has been operated in the country. Chemisal will be replaced by vineyards, and chaparral by fruit trees, and the formerly barren plain will "Blossom as the rose." It will be one of the most beautiful settlements in Los Angeles county, or any other portion of Southern California.

A February 26, 1889 *Los Angeles Times* advertisement for fifteen acres in Watt's Subdivision of San Rafael touted its advantages:

5½ m. Los Angeles, 18 m. from ocean; 1 m. from depot; ½ m. from school, and 1 m. from church; soil—sandy loam; valley; suited for grain, fruit and vegetables; water supply, Verdugo canon, piped on land; water shares go with land; house and stable, $700; growing crops, fruit trees, strawberries, potatoes and barley; $425. per acre; warranty deed; 1/8 cash balance in 1 and 2 years; 10 per cent.

Eighteen miles from the ocean? I think not, but this gives a good picture of costs and crops raised.

TURNER RANCH

The top part of Rancho San Rafael that is now part of the Flintridge section of La Cañada Flintridge were Lots 95, 94, and 93. Lots 95 and 94 to the west were purchased by Edson Silas Turner, a neighbor in Pasadena of Charles H. Watts. Lot 93 was the easternmost lot bordering Rancho San Pasqual, ending just west of the Arroyo Seco, buyer unknown.

The Turner Ranch property consisted of Lot 95 (186.08 acres) and Lot 94 (618.15 acres) for a total of 804.23 acres. It bordered what is now Chevy Chase Drive to the east and to the south of Berkshire Avenue, which is the border between Rancho La Cañada to the north and Rancho San Rafael.

A deed for the transaction has not been found—not even a newspaper notice. This was during the land boom of the 1880s in California and was a time of frenetic buying and flipping properties and forming different consortiums; it makes locating deeds quite difficult. Turner most likely purchased the property in 1883 or 1884 and, according to his son, Edson Jr., paid $4,000 for the property.

A recent history stated that the property was purchased from Glassell and Chapman; however, they were awarded Rancho La Cañada in the Great Partition of 1871. A 1953 *Pasadena News Press* article noted that the Turner Ranch was located north of Devil's Gate Dam. Devil's Gate Dam is located on the Arroyo Seco and is part of Pasadena. North of the dam is Jet Propulsion Laboratory, located in La Cañada, and that was part of Rancho La Cañada, so it is doubtful that they lived there, but perhaps nearby. The dam area was popular with young people in the early days for picnics and day trips. The dam was not constructed until 1921.

The dividing line between Rancho San Pasqual and Rancho San Rafael goes right through the middle of the Devil's Gate Dam area; the southern dividing line is west of Linda Vista.

EDSON SILAS TURNER

Edson Silas Turner was a Pasadena businessman and civic leader. Although not an 1874 founding member of the California Colony of Indiana, a farmers' cooperative limited to fifty families, he joined in 1875. The original name morphed into the Indiana Colony, then the Southern California Orange Growers Association and finally, in 1886, at the insistence of the postmaster, Pasadena. The family came here in 1875, as detailed in Mrs. Esther Turner's 1927 obituary:

> *In 1875, her husband Edson Turner, and her three sons, Edson, Charles and Bruce left Illinois where they had lived for nearly twenty-five years, to come to the West and Pasadena. Their first house was a shack on a waste stretch of land, which afterward became known as the Turner Tract, west of Fair Oaks and north of Walnut, the house standing on what now is Cypress avenue.*
>
> *After some years, the house on Walnut street, facing Cypress, was built, and it was there that Mrs. Turner lived until a few years ago. Old age necessitated her living with her son at 303 Cypress avenue, which house is, however, on the original tract of land acquired in the early days, the family having the distinction of living where they first settled for more than fifty years.*

Their house was located near the onramp of the 210 freeway on Walnut Avenue, west of Fair Oaks.

Edson was born in Walworth, New York, in 1838 and was a Civil War veteran. On August 27, 1862, at twenty-four years old, he enlisted for three years in the Eighty-sixth Regiment, Illinois Infantry, as a corporal. This regiment saw much action, including at the Battle of Chickamauga, and he served under General Hood as part of Sherman's march to Atlanta. He was wounded at the battle at Peachtree Creek on July 19, 1864, and was sent to a hospital, which was not exactly a good experience at that time. He was discharged in Washington, D.C., on June 6, 1865, and on August 29, 1865, he applied for an invalid pension. His Civil War record describes him as five feet, seven and a half inches tall with dark hair, dark eyes and dark complexion; his occupation is listed as farmer. Edson was engaged to Esther Eby when he enlisted, and after he returned from the war, they were married on January 13, 1866.

After Turner purchased the ranch property, he built a home as a second residence, did some farming and had caretakers or tenants working there. He probably was going to develop the property and sell off some of it, but in 1887, the land boom was bottoming out, and by 1888, it was over. Tragically, Turner died in a horse accident when he was fifty years old, according to a report from the January 15, 1889 *Los Angeles Times*:

> *Pasadena, Jan. 14—*
> *A SAD DEATH*
>
> *Councilman Turner was the victim of an awful death this morning. At about 9 o'clock he left home in his buggy for the Raymond station, where he was to meet some relatives by street car. He had crossed the track of the California Central Railroad, and in attempting to recross in order to accustom the animal to the escaping steam and noise of the locomotive, he was thrown out of the buggy and dashed against a signal post. The animal, frightened and driverless, made a dash for liberty, completely wrecking the buggy. Mr. Turner was almost instantly killed, the blood oozing from his mouth and ears. His head was badly mangled and the brains were scattered promiscuously about. The injured man was taken to his home at the corner of Fair Oaks avenue and Walnut street, and medical aid summoned. Life, however, was of short duration, death relieving him of his sufferings within half an hour afterward.*
>
> *Deceased was in his fiftieth year and a man of family. He has a son who is now a student at the State University. For many years he has been*

La Cañada in 1888. *Courtesy of La Cañada Congregational Church photography collection at Lanterman Museum Archives.*

a member of the City Council, and was chairman of several committees in that body. As a mark of respect the Council Chamber has been draped.

Mr. Turner was an old resident here and had accumulated considerable property. He was a member of the lodge of A.O.U.W. and of the Grand Army.

The funeral will in all probability take place from his late residence on Wednesday.

On January 17, 1889, the *Los Angeles Times* reported the following:

FINAL RITES

The last funeral rites of the late Councilman, Edson Turner, who was the victim of an awfully sad death, took place this afternoon. The remains, in charge of the A.O.U.W. lodge, were escorted from the family residence on North Fair Oaks avenue to the Presbyterian Church, followed by John F. Godfrey Post of the Grand Army of the Republic and Phil Kearney Camp, Sons of Veterans.

At the church very impressive services were held, and the attendance of friends was very large. The casket was loaded with beautiful floral offerings, and a pillow of snowy-white flowers had incrested in heliotropes the initials "E.T." The choir of the church sang several beautiful selections appropriate to the occasion. Rev. M.N. Cornelius preached a very impressive sermon, referring to the character of the deceased, and filled with regret that his own last days in our city should be saddened by the death of a friend whom he well knew and beloved. Other remarks were made by the Rev. D.D. Hill, pastor of the Congregational Church. The remains were interred in the cemetery in North Pasadena.

Aftermath

A review of Turner's probate file at the Huntington Library archives indicates that other than a small stipend to a niece, he left his entire estate to his wife, Esther Eby Turner. In addition to the Turner Ranch, he left her properties in Long Beach and Pasadena, as well as Rancho San Pasqual, San Bernardino, Rancho Los Cerritos and Garvanza. She managed the properties quite well, was very socially prominent and continued to operate the ranch property. A November 19, 1889 *Los Angeles Times* article recounted the travails of a caretaker on the property:

Mrs. Courtright of La Cañada, whose husband skipped out six weeks ago, has since had a weary existence, has farmed it on the Turner ranch, with the aid of her daughter of 16. She has another daughter of 4. The mother and oldest daughter have carried on the ranch and managed to make a living. Courtright left numerous debts behind. Not a word has been heard from him since he left.

At the time of Edson's death, the eldest son, Charles, was already in college and would become a well-known artist with no interest in farming or living in Pasadena. Sons Charles (eighteen) and Ed (sixteen) managed the ranch, and it was a place of many social gatherings, including mandolin parties, which were the rage in the late nineteenth century. Ed was the only family member who lived at the ranch on a permanent basis, moving there after his marriage in April 1900 to Tina Fisk. They lived there for several years, and all three of their daughters were born on the ranch. Following is an amusing story from *La Crescenta: Sources of History*, contributed by John O. Slutman and Dan W. Green:

FARM IN FLINTRIDGE

Whenever we drive through beautiful Flintridge, we are reminded of the days when the central area there comprised the 660 acres of the Ed Turner Ranch. It was largely raw land, some small acreage was used for grain land and the remainder was just pasture. It was the home of Turner's "Community Bull" and for many years before Senator Flint bought the property for $12,500, it was well known for the bull. In his old age the animal became intractable and many of our farmers learned at first hand of his irritability. One of the writers of this comment had an experience in this regard with the beast and had it not been for the expert handling of pitchforks in the bull's corral by Ed Turner, this column would have had only one author. (Ed Turner, incidentally, lives now near Portland, Oregon, where he has a ranch and two bulls.)

An August 1904 *Los Angeles Times* article about bee conditions that year reported that the Turner Ranch had sixty-five hives to help pollinate the 665 acres all in fruit. In 1905, Ed and family toured Oregon in a covered wagon and bought a ranch in Fort Klamath. They returned to Pasadena, moving to Oregon permanently the next year. With Ed moving away, Mrs. Turner sold the ranch property to Frank Flint for $25,000. From the October 20, 1905 *Los Angeles Herald*:

SENATOR FLINT BUYS RANCH

It was Senator Frank Flint of Los Angeles who purchased last week the magnificent Edson Turner ranch at La Canyada and not Senator Dorsey, as predicted at that time. Senator Dorsey it appears was the agent in the deal, but the property was for Mr. Flint and will eventually become the senator's home. Senator Flint will not locate on his new purchase this season, since he is going to be in Washington for the winter, but when he returns in the spring the handsome ranch will be put in condition for his occupancy. The Edson Turner ranch lies just north of Devil's gate and extends into the Arroyo on the west, and is a charming location for the handsome residence to be erected there. Its recent transfer was at the state price of $25,000.

The deed, recorded and signed by Esther Turner, is found in Book 2437 at the Los Angeles County Recorders Office in Norwalk, California, and dated November 2, 1905. It grants the property not to Frank Flint but to the State Loan & Investment Company for the magnificent sum of $10. This is another example of the puzzling real estate transactions of the early days (and maybe present day, too). The only description of the property is referenced in the aforementioned June 1883 subdivision map and does not indicate the exact acreage. Turner had sold off some of his property in Lots 94 and 95; one notable sale was fifteen acres in Lot 95 to Jacob Lanterman in April 1885 for $300.

A MECCA OF SOCIETY

Frank Putnam Flint was born in 1862 in Massachusetts and moved with his family to San Francisco in 1869 and to Los Angeles in 1887. He was a deputy United States marshal for four years, was admitted to the bar in 1892 and practiced law. He was an assistant United States attorney, a judge of the superior court of Los Angeles county and the United States district attorney for the southern district of California from 1897 to 1901. In 1905, the same year he purchased the Turner Ranch, he was elected as a Republican to the United States Senate. He served one six-year term, choosing not to run for reelection, as he was convinced that he did not have enough support to be reelected.

During the period when he served as a senator, he lived most of the time in Washington, D.C., and did not start developing his Flintridge property until after he left office in 1911. He bought more acreage in the area and built a replica of a southern governor's mansion in 1914 on Flintridge Avenue as a secondary residence, maintaining his home in Pasadena as his primary residence. The Flintridge home was sold in 1929 and demolished by the new owner.

Flint spent an estimated $200,000 in subdivision improvements. A few homes near his residence had already been built, but the tract was officially opened for sale in January 1917, as recounted in this January 14, 1917 *Los Angeles Times* article:

> *Famous Tract to Be Opened*
> *Flintridge Will Go Way of Other Land Domains.*
> *Sightly Holding to Be Made into Home Area.*
> *Miles of Scenic Boulevards Built by Owner.*

Flintridge, the well-known property of former United States Senator Frank P. Flint in La Canada Valley, is to go the way of other great suburban land holdings in the vicinity of Los Angeles. Announcement is made that the entire 1500 acres comprised within the tract will at once be placed upon the market.

Mr. Flint acquired 700 acres of the sightly estate in 1905, this part of the property having formerly been a stock ranch. The rest was purchased in parcels of varying size. The owner began taking steps looking to the subdivision of the acreage about six years ago. Since that time close to $200,000 has been expended in general improvements.

Five miles of scenic boulevards, with curbs and gutters, have been constructed in the tract, and these have been lined with trees. The land is largely covered with oaks, sycamores, eucalyptus and pines, and the surveys have been carried out so as to avoid any marring of the natural beauties of the holding. Each roadway opens its own picturesque and beautiful vista, one of the finest bits of road being a winding drive leading high into the hills on the south side of the valley back of Mr. Flint's own country home.

The owner has cut the property into plots of from one to forty acres in size. The sites thus laid out are of varying topography, some being on knolls and hillsides and others comparatively level. The landscapers in charge of the development have so laid out boundary lines as to give each different building site its quota of trees, with an outlook over the valley and toward the Sierra Madres Mountains.

The announcement of the final opening of Flintridge is important not only on account of the magnitude and scope of the project, but as an indication of the great improvement in business and financial conditions. The enterprise is one of the largest in the history of suburban real estate around Los Angeles, the tract being probably the biggest high-class residential subdivision ever put on the market in this vicinity. The owner has been waiting for a propitious time in which to carry out his plans.

Mr. Flint's own home occupies one of the charming hillside sites of Flintridge, its grounds comprising about fifteen acres.

The various newspaper accounts, deeds and recollections have led to many differing statements about the exact size of the Turner Ranch: 660 acres, 700 acres and 980 acres have all been reported. From the subdivision map, we know that the original purchase was for 804 acres; some acreage was sold off. The exact number of acres purchased by Flint's agent is not known, but it was probably closer to the oft-reported 700 acres.

Flintridge was developed and always intended to be an upscale community, with large homes and lots, riding clubs and other exclusive amenities. Flint himself envisioned the development as, and I quote, a "Mecca for Society." Whether he was trying to maximize his profit or was just an insufferable snob is a subject for speculation, but he did achieve his goal. Flintridge remains an extremely upscale community. It was incorporated into the town of La Cañada in 1976 and has the second-longest city name in the United States: La Cañada Flintridge.

CHAPTER 7

CULTURE AND POETRY IN THE VALLEY

In the early days of settlement in the Crescenta Valley, people were very isolated. A trip into Los Angeles took, on a good day, at least one hour going and two hours coming back. Going to newly established Pasadena, one had to cross the Arroyo Seco—in rainy weather, this could be a treacherous endeavor. It was not until the Arroyo Seco bridge was built and opened in May 1893 that getting to Pasadena was made much easier.

The early settlers had to make a social life and entertain themselves in this rural area. Just because people were farming in an isolated place did not mean that they went without cultural pursuits. Many of the people were educated and well read. In fact, people before the invention of television were generally much more social than we are today, with all our technology that gets us connected to the world without having to leave home and interact with other people face to face. Writing poetry was one popular pastime.

DR. BENJAMIN AND MRS. CAROLINE BRIGGS

Dr. Benjamin B. Briggs was the developer of La Crescenta. He and his second wife, Caroline Crane Briggs, lived at their large agricultural property, which they called the Terrace, settling in La Crescenta in 1884. The home had many visitors and social functions. The following two poems are dated September 2,

1890, and are in Caroline Crane Briggs's handwriting (from the manuscript collection of Caroline Crane Briggs letters, located at the Huntington Library Archives and used with its permission). Dr. Briggs passed away in 1893:

Dr. Briggs

And he wandered away, x away
With Nature the dear old nurse
Who sang to him night x day
The shyness of the universe
And [word illegible] *the way seemed long*

Or his heart began to fail,
She would sing a more wonderful song

Or tell a more wonderful tale.
So she keeps him still a child
And will not let him go,
Though at times his heart
beats wild
For the field of Long Ago

Mrs. Keeler

Who can find an excellent woman? She hath not the Curse of idleness
She considereth the field and buyeth it—with the fruit of her hands she planteth a vineyard
Then shall we drink this draft of herbs, part sweet and part slip.

LITERARY AND SOCIAL SOCIETIES

George Crane was the nephew of Dr. Benjamin B. Briggs, the founder of La Crescenta. George was the editor of the Crescenta Literary Society. In commemoration of an attendance of eight of Crescenta's young people to the La Cañada Literary Society the evening of November 30, 1894, he wrote

Tea party at Granite Heights on April 14, 1899, from Allie Bathey's 1902 photo album.

Foothill scene painted by Winifred Bathey, circa 1902.

the following poem. The young people were George Crane, Emily Scherb, Lottie Pettit, Matie Williams, Will Williams, Allie Bathey, Winifred Bathey and Herbert Bathey, driven over to La Cañada in Mr. Bathey's father's "spring wagon." The Batheys and George Crane were Presbyterians and did not believe in dancing; they were most likely meeting at the La Canada Elementary School:

To the La Canada Literary
Eight of us did go,
To hear the nasal secretary
Read the minutes rather slow.

Four little girls began to sing
A piece about a blister,
That made the house with applause ring;
Ah! If I only had a sister.

A speaking was the next on the program,
By Velix or his twin;
And this is the way it ran
Something about the earth or sin.

Miss Hunsaker a solo sang,
Which made La Crescenta sorrow;
For Loud Canada's voices rang
For our home talent to borrow.

The fireworks came with their Light
Also with their smell,
To show two little girls in White,
Our girls can't swing so well.

Then there came a pantomime
Behind the curtain white;
Where the boy kicked the lion
Between us and the light.

The quartet gave us a beautiful song
Accompanied by the organ,
How Mary and Martha had just gone long,
And a Negro in the sorghum.

Then Mr. Whitney a lecture gave free
To them who around him sat,
How that dancing should not be
In a public place like that.

Then we were treated to a surprise
With its popcorn and candies,
When the chairman did arise
And thank the Canada dandies.

The Roadrunner

Even in isolated La Crescenta, schoolchildren had creative outlets. The *Los Angeles Herald* sponsored writing contests for schoolchildren in the West. Edith Bathey, daughter of Charles and Mary Bathey, whose ranch property remains intact at the top of Briggs and Shields Avenue, won first place in a 1901 contest. She was fourteen years old at the time:

Edyth L. Bathey, La Crescenta, Cal., Class A., $2.00
Katherine Hanson, Riverside, Cal. $2.00
Mildreth E. Hughes, Globe, A.T. (Arizona Territory), Class C., $1.00

The Roadrunner
By Edythe L. Bathey, Class A. Fourteen Years

While sitting in the house recently I heard a cooing, like that of a dove. I did not pay much attention at first, but it came nearer and nearer, so I went out to see what made the noise. I did not see it at first, so I began to mock it as near as possible.

I soon saw a roadrunner standing in the shade of an orange tree and making this queer noise. He would bend his head forward till his bill nearly

Edith Bathey wrangling the family mules at the gate to their ranch at the top of Briggs and Shields in La Crescenta.

touched the ground, let his long tail droop and move the body up and down by bending at the knees.

He must have been calling his mate for he would call and run on to the next tree, look at his feet, get farther in the shade and call again. There was a quail near him under another tree, and he ran at it as if he were going to fight it.

After he had called again and again I saw another roadrunner coming toward him with a snake in its bill. It also ran from tree to tree to get in the shade but did not call for fear the snake would fall. Soon the one that did not have the snake saw me and gave a danger cry that sounded like the rattles boys have in Fiestas, made of hard wood. When the one with the snake heard the cry it ran away and either hid the snake or ate it, for I saw it afterwards without it.

The roadrunner is about the size of a two-months old turkey, with a long bill that serves as a knife. His tail is long and steers him when he is sailing along the roads. They eat snakes and lizards. They catch rattlesnakes by corralling them in with cactus leaves.

California Songs

Reuben Alexander Slaven Wade was born in Virginia in 1847. His family moved to Missouri, and he worked on the family farm and as a telephone operator. By 1900, he had moved to Santa Ana, California, working as a real estate agent. In 1909, he was living in Los Angeles, where he worked as an oil and mine broker and a part-time poet. In 1930, he was widowed and living at 4310 Briggs Avenue in La Crescenta.

The following poem appears in his privately published 1909 collection of poems, *California Songs* (there is no music in it despite its name). It is in a typical romantic style of the day—there is no mention of fires, floods or mudslides:

La Canada

Have you been to the vale
Sweeping up from Glendale
When the wind blew a gale
In wild La Canada?
Have you wandered at will
When the night wind was still
And your heart was a thrill
In the vale, La Canada?
Have you sat half asleep
Where the shadows were deep
When the summer nights sweep
O'er dark La Canada?
Oh! the fairest that grows
Is the soft-tinted rose,
When the summer wind blows
In bright La Canada.
There the flowers never die;
There the mountains are high,
And their peaks touch the sky

Around La Canada.
There the soul is at rest,
And the spirit is blest
In the vale we love best,
In dear La Canada.
And the day and night seem
To glide by like a dream
Where the softest moonbeam
Falls on La Canada.
There is nought that will cloy,
There's no trace of alloy
In that valley of joy,
The sweet La Canada.
'Tis an unhappy day
When the sad heart must say,
As it wanders away:
"Farewell! La Canada!"
There the piteous wail
Of the unmated quail
Strikes the heart like a flail
In fair La Canada.
There the mocking bird trills
All the music that thrills
The glad heart in the hills
'Round dear La Canada.
And the turtle doves greet
Their fair mates when they meet
With their cooings so sweet
In sweet La Canada.
And the lights of Mount Lowe
In the summer nights glow
Where the wildflowers blow
By fair La Canada.
There the splendor enthralls,
And the light grandly falls
On the Gould castle walls,
By fair La Canada.
Oh! the mist-shrouded hills
And the grandeur that fills

Every heart till it thrills
In fair La Canada.
Not a sad bell may toll;
Not a shadow may roll
O'er the undisturbed soul,
In calm La Canada.
There no tear dims the eye
And no heart heaves a sigh
Where the summer birds fly
In fair La Canada.
And no mortal may weep
Where the silent years sleep,
As the centuries sweep
O'er fair La Canada.

The Crescenta Valley was a hub for invalid sanitariums; all are gone now. One of the largest, Kimball Sanitarium, was demolished in 1960, and Merritt Kimball's scrapbook was saved from a dumpster. This poem was most likely written by a patient there; it shows the isolation from family and friends and the hopelessness of the patients:

Oh! You are here to stay as long as you should
If you do for freedom feel the move
To escape, there's no chance on the card,
For the doors are locked so carefully
And the windows with wire are barred.

You can search for a pass
To get through the glass,
But it's not worthwhile at least;
For being a human, you are too large
To get out, like any small beast.

When you ask why the wires on the window stand
You are told by a nurse with a look so bland
"It's to keep out the flies that bug us so."
And you are green enough to think it is true,
But for the fact that you still do not know.
For the truth is this, from one that is wise;

Their purpose you really can judge from their size.
While the flies they do keep out very well,
It's the bugs inside that they restrain.

R.E.D. June 9, 1927

Community Bulletin

The *Community Bulletin* of La Cañada Valley was published on the first and third Fridays of each month, except in July and August, by the Congregational (Community) Church of La Canada Valley.

Emily Lanterman was the wife of Dr. Roy Lanterman (son of the founder of La Cañada), the son of Jacob and Ammoretta Lanterman. Emily and Roy built their dream home in La Cañada in 1915 and called it El Retiro (the Retreat). The home is on the National Register of Historic Places and is operated as a museum by the City of La Cañada Flintridge. Although no one can say for sure, it is believed that the trail from the San Gabriel Mission to the San Fernando Mission wended its way through La Cañada. Emily C. Lanterman wrote the following in January 4, 1935:

La Canada

In a sunny Southland valley
Winds a trail the Padres trod
When they journeyed between the missions
On a pilgrimage for God.

Cool winds from the Sierra Madres
Toss back gods from the San Rafaels
Sighing through swaying oak trees, arias
Low, and clear as vesper bells.

The patterns cast on the pathways
By the lacily woven leaves
Dance merrily with the sun's rays
In mid-summer ecstasies.

Stilled the calls of gay vaqueros
Silent the ox carts whine
Only the purr of speeding autos
Whirring past in an endless line.

Disturb the peaceful noon-day hour
With sounds of a later day.
When minions of progress and power
Wafted the pueblos into cities gay.

There's a rush of wings o'er my patio
The fountain accompanies the lay
That birds trill 'round El Retiro
A jubilant song of today.

Scrolls in mission archives reveal
This joyous theme was an anthem, when
Padre and Indian felt the appeal
Of nature's lure in this mountain glen.

In this glen where heaven speaks
At murmuring dawn, to whispers of night,
With rose-hued light on the mountain peaks
Limning our homes in a dream-land site.

The fading trail in the valley
Now joins a great highway
Where friend ceaselessly toils for friend,
To this mystery at the journey's end.

Shadows creep up my patio wall
Dead leaves wrinkle, then crumple and fail,
But the life of courage and joy within
Leads us through winter to spring again.

THE LA CRESCENTA FLOOD

After a devastating fire in the foothills in November 1933, a great flood was released in La Crescenta on New Year's Day in 1934. It caused much death and devastation. Many people moved away and never came back. Grace Lawrence Harper was fifty-two and living at 4911 Castle Road, La Crescenta, when the November 1933 fire and the 1934 New Year's Day flood ravaged the foothills. Grace was a widow. Her home was wiped out, and she moved to Glendale with her daughter, supporting herself by giving piano lessons. She never moved back to La Crescenta. This powerful poem was published in the *Ledger* newspaper shortly thereafter:

Our Beloved Hills

Nude I lie, Stripped of all my verdant beauty,
Scarred by fire, forced with flood,
Oh, that I might hide my plight.

Nude I lie, Scorned and feared by those I love,
Bruised by fire, seamed by flood,
Oh! That I might hide my plight.

Nude I lie, Shamed am I,
Cover me, Oh! Sons of Noah,
Cover me, and hide my plight.

Kate H. Wright was fifty-four, single and living with her sister, Clara, in Glendale in 1934 when she wrote this poem about the fire and flood:

The Flood

How oft have we heard the story of the wonderful works of Man!
He has conquered Time and Distance with his swift-flying ships of the sky,
From the air he has snatched the music of the trilling pipes of Pan,
In arrogance, he even dares Dame Nature to defy!

In spite of all the marvels the hand of Man has wrought,
He yet stands impotent before the fury of flood and fire,
No matter with what courage these great Forces may be
Fought,
They leave in their path destruction, inevitable and dire.

The high, protecting mountains that stand above the plain,
Are now all bare and denuded from Fire's devastating Sweep,
No soft-covering chaparral, nor tree, holds back the Winter rain,
That sends a destroying torrent down the canons, black and deep.

All night the rain came down, came down from a leaden sky,
All day it fell with steady force, the torrent never
Ceased,
Rain fell in the valley and lowlands, rain fell in the mountains high,
The gates of Heaven were opened, and the Flood Gods were released.

Lights gleamed forth from the windows of little homes, snug
And warm,
Music and laughter mingled with the sound of descending rain;
For a New Year was coming in, borne on the wings of the
Storm,
The old year with its want and sadness was swiftly on the wane.

Suddenly, out of the darkness, an angry, sullen roar
Was borne to the ears of the watchers, above the music
Gay,
Over homes, and trees, and landscapes, mad waters began to pour,
Mid boulders and surging black torrent, all in ruins lay.

Waters rushed down from the canons, carrying precious soil,
Torn from the bosom of Mother Earth, leaving her gashed and scarred;
Trees were uprooted, and crashed in that black and horrid
Turmoil,
Floods of dark water descended on all that its way had Barred.

Gone were the lights in the houses, the sound of music was
Stilled,
Only the raging waters were mingled with awful din
Of screaming, struggling people, with which the wild night was filled.
Leaving naught but wreckage where happy homes had
Been.

Night, and the storm, and the darkness, waters rushing by,
In spite of Man's puny efforts, Nature will have her way.
Rain-drenched Dawn at last reveals homes that in ruins lie,
Friends and loved ones gone to a nobler, happier day.

When will Man ever learn to forsake his careless ways?
The inevitable lesson know, that flood always follows
Fire,
Destruction ever follows when Nature's law he disobeys,
An leaves him naught but ruin, where once was
Heart's Desire.

Fire that spreads desolation, drops from one man a careless Hand,
But scores of victims suffer who are innocent of offense
Changed is a verdant valley, to a waste of desert sand,
Prey to the wild Winter wind, and the Summer's heat
Intense.

CHAPTER 8

Charles F. Pate, Valley Chronicler and Photographer

Arriving in La Cañada in 1893, Charles F. Pate was not one of the earliest pioneers in the Valley. He acknowledged this in his manuscript "Reminiscences of a Tenderfoot": "I notice that I am sometimes referred to as a 'Pioneer.' If this be so I am only a j.g. as the real pioneers predate me from one or two decades: they were the real 'Rude forefathers of the hamlet.'"

Charlie Pate settled permanently in La Cañada, was an avid photographer and wrote extensively of early Valley history. He was born on March 7, 1874, in Eltham, Kent, England, the oldest surviving son of Peter Pate, a marble merchant, and Jane Hicks Oliver. He had an older brother, Arthur William, who died before Charlie was born; two sisters, Mary Alice and Florence; and a younger brother, Walter Stewart.

He appears to have been on very good terms with his parents and siblings and did not leave England under a cloud of controversy or due to the lack of an inheritance. He traveled to Glendora to work at a ranch that a school chum had arrived at a few months earlier.

At the age of eighteen, Pate left Liverpool, England, on December14, 1892, aboard the SS *Teutonic* of the White Star Line, arriving at the Port of New York late on December 21, 1892; he left the ship the next day. He traveled second class, which meant that he was processed for immigration aboard ship and not on Ellis Island, which only processed third-class passengers. He had four bags, and his destination was listed as Glendora, California. In 1947, he wrote of his travels from England to California; his writings give an excellent picture of international travel in the late nineteenth century:

Coming to America
by Charles Pate

As a sort of preface to the actual history I will tell of the event which is responsible for my being here at all and refer you to the date of 13th Dec. 1892. On this day my father & I left London by midnight train and arrived at Liverpool before 6 a.m. in weather which Charles Dickens' Mr. McCawber would have described as "damp, moist and unpleasant."

S.S. Teutonic of the White Star Line was a giant in those days, 10,000. tons. We went out on a tender about noon & it was with a sinking heart that I watched this boat bearing my beloved father to the shore whilst I myself was on my way to a strange land and new experiences. After leaving Queenstown, we were soon out on the Atlantic with its winter weather. A crash early one morning announced the washing away of a life boat. Apparently everyone within ear-shot was paying enforced tribute to the Sea god: seasickness replaced home-sickness.

I was one of four in a cabin…I have on several occasions been inspired by the sight of a kilted regiment swinging along with their pipes at their head. When, however, an aggressive Scotsman sits in an upper berth & pipes to a lot of people who are too sick to either slay him or to puncture his wretched instrument, well, that is something else. I am not sure but that the pipes were an antidote for seasickness: one misery at a time.

The voyage in general was the usual routine of an Atlantic crossing: concerts, sweepstakes, and so on. We cast anchor late on the night of 21st December. I had my first glimpse of N.Y. by the dawn's early light next morning. There were no rocket's red glare or bombs bursting in air but there was a glorious sun-rise. I had never before experienced such bitter cold.

I was met at the dock by a business connection of my father. He showed me some of the chief points of interest in the city & helped me on my way.

After traveling anywhere in England with only a small piece of pasteboard for a ticket, I was considerable surprised when in exchange for my travel voucher, I received about six feet of paper: in the ensuing days, how I did watch that strip growing gradually shorter as we approached the journey's end.

Although not occupying a sleeping-berth, travel had been comfortable enough till we reached Ogden where, after a 2 hour wait, I transferred to an emigrant coach—all that my ticket called for. The car was dirty &

so were the occupants who presented a fair cross-section of the world's underprivileged classes...The floor was covered with straw—an invitation to scratch: chickens are not the only beings that scratch.

The seats were of hard-wood half-round slats & were so constructed as to allow two opposite seats to slide together. When the two backs lay flat they formed a sleeping platform. A friendly man & I pooled our resources & slept as best we could: the impression of the slats lasted for some time. Other impressions were the passage through the 48 miles of snow sheds and finally that of coming out of the snow and descending to the orange groves of Sacramento.

The river was high & there was some doubt as the safety of the trestle, but we made it & I was just in time to swing aboard a train as it commended to pull out for Los Angeles. Glendora being my final destination, I got off at Alosta (AZUSA) & drove to Glendora with the mail-carrier & was picked up by my future boss & conveyed to his ranch at the foot of the mountains. It was most cheering there to be greeted my old (school) chum, Ted, who had preceded me to California a few months earlier & whose letters were the determining factor in my decision to come to Southern California.

So this very young (18) & very green Englishman commenced a new life and commenced to accumulate impressions & experiences.

I experienced my first Norther a few days after my arrival. The boss, who was of a very serious mind, was desirous that a couple of 18 year old kids should promptly "Put away childish things and become men." He was much displeased because we greeted with laughter the overturning of a small building (by said Norther) which was useless when in a recumbent position.

I forgot to state that I did not come to the U.S.A. on a lecture: when there was any lecturing done, I was on the receiving end.

LA CAÑADA

After a few months, Pate left Glendora and settled in La Cañada, arriving in June 1893, one month after the opening of the Arroyo Seco bridge; he did not take pictures of the opening ceremonies, as is sometimes suggested:

Pate (right, with guitar) and friend Ben Johnson (with mandolin). Their leather leggings were for protection against rattlesnakes. *Courtesy of La Cañada Congregational Church photography collection at Lanterman Museum Archives.*

Early Days in La Canada

Dec. 12, 1892—Voyage to America. Reached Needhams of Glendora a few days before 1st Jan. 1893. Stayed there till the later part of June and then came to Lantermans at La Canada and stayed there till the end of 1893. First met Watermans whilst there, they having recently returned from the North. Bached with Tom Sawyer [a fellow Brit] *in La Canada for several months in a house just W. of McArthur store in 1894.*

He and I bought 5 acre lot 9, Hillard Tract in partnership that spring and planted the orchard in April. Pettit built the house for us that year. My father had advanced the purchase money.

The partnership proved to be unsatisfactory, and as Tom was not prepared to pay his share of the interest, I decided to terminate it. Dad had drawn up an agreement for arbitration in case of dispute. After having disposed of our personal financial matters, Tom claimed a share in the increase in the value of the property. I invoked the above agreement and chose Rob Waterman to represent me; Tom chose D.J. Green, and they selected Judge Carnahan as the third member of the board. The decision went against Tom, & there the matter ended.

Clearing land on Briggs Avenue for Santos in Dec. 1894 and Jan. 1895, Rob and I tented on the ground. Steve Velix came on the job after Rob hurt his eyes. Helped to move Judge Carnahan's effects from his ranch to the old Williams house. He later moved into the Charley Germain house on Indiana Street and from there to Bert Williams house where he died in 1907.

Planted pumpkins between my young orchard trees. Tom Sawyer married Ada Burgess in 1895 and moved on to Squires' place, on old Canon road, below the Petit place. Watermans built their first house on their 10 acres—afterwards (1914) Dr. Eversole's.

I believe that it was in 1894 that I first visited Switzer's Camp, taking Mr. Huckley, one of Dunham's boarders, with me. I went out from there with Johnny Simmons to his house in Las Casitas. We went down the Arroyo and crossed into Millard Canyon and so on down. This may have been in 1895.

Land Winston was frozen to death at Buckhorn 9th Nov. 1893. I believe that Watermans worked at Switzers the summer of 1894.

The Angeles National Forest was a popular hunting, hiking and camping destination for Valley residents. Don Carpenter (*Ledger* publisher) encouraged Pate to write down his recollections of Valley history and his visits to Switzer's Camp in the forest:

Notes on Old Switzer's Camp

After a recent visit to Switzer's Camp in the company of Don Carpenter, and the perusal of the present camp Scrap Book kindly lent to me by Mr. Swanson, it has occurred to me that it may be of interest if the Scrap Book contains some additional notes concerning the old camp as I first knew it in 1894–97.

As noted in the record, the original burro corral was located a short distance below Las Casitas and the stage from Pasadena delivered camp guests to this point.

In 1894 or 1895 the corral was located a short distance above the present ranger station which is at the foot of what was formerly known as "Brunks Grade," a narrow wagon road leading from the Arroyo Seco to La Canada.

At the corral was an abandoned cabin (the name of the owner escapes me). The next cabin was inhabited by the Barker family and further up was "The old W.W. Whitney Place," later known as "The Hahn Place." Whitney was one of the early settlers in La Canada—his 10 acres being well up and on the west side of Palm Drive, or as it was then called,

Old Switzer's Camp in the 1890s. It was run by Rob and Libby Waterman. Here Libby is the woman standing on the left, and Rob is standing up fifth from the left with supplies. Waterman Mountain is named after them. *Courtesy of La Cañada Congregational Church photography collection at Lanterman Museum Archives.*

Dunham Avenue, and adjoined the property where Judge Avery later resided.

Getting back now to the Arroyo: the last cabin was at the junction of the Arroyo and Dark Canon. It was of logs and was built by Godfrey of the Pasadena Water Company.

From the corral the guests, either afoot or burro-back, followed the winding trail in the bottom of the canon for 4 miles to Vail's Camp, a small flat alongside the creek.

From Vail's Camp a short ascent followed by an abrupt turn and a short descent, carried the trail around the falls at the mouth of Long Canon to the south bank of that canon and then commenced 1½ miles of leg-breaking zig-zags to a large Manzanita tree on the ridge. This marked one mile from Camp. The first trail had followed the ups and downs of this ridge from the Arroyo—mostly "ups." After the One Miles tree came "Hard Scrabble," a steep descent and an equally steep ascent, the trail being cut in the bare face of the cliff. From this point there was an easy, winding grade to the Camp. Immediately before dropping down to the Camp a couple of narrow rock gullies necessitated "bridges," these consisting of a pine log on the outer edge and cross logs resting on them and on the rock of the cliff. The logs were covered with broken rock and soil and each time that repairs were made on the bridges each burro would smell and investigate before crossing.

Pate at his house in La Cañada in 1902 with his dog, Roxie. A typical bachelor residence, it has three doorways and only one set of stairs. *Courtesy of La Cañada Congregational Church photography collection at Lanterman Museum Archives.*

Pate built his home on his Hillard property in 1894. He planted peaches and French prune trees, reveled in the hunting parties at the Hall Ranch and became good friends with the younger Tom Hall, as well as Rob and Libby Waterman (of Mount Waterman). Pate went back on a visit to England in 1897.

On July 30, 1903, he married Mary Edith Wilbur, a local teacher, in La Cañada. In 1911, she was one of the founders of the Parent-Teacher Association of La Cañada and served as president of the La Cañada Thursday Club. She soon became pregnant, prompting a trip to England in 1904. According to local postmaster Edwin Cooper, the reason for the trip was that if the baby was a boy, it would be in line for inheritance, and they wanted to make sure that it was an English birth.

The baby was a girl, Mary Florence (who went by Florence), most likely named after his two sisters. This was the Pates' only child.

Charles's occupations were many, as a five-acre ranch could not have supported three people so easily. Various censuses and other records indicate that he was an apricot pickier, rancher, farmer, carpenter and a line layer

Roxie, a much-loved dog. *Courtesy of La Cañada Congregational Church photography collection at Lanterman Museum Archives.*

in San Pedro during World War I. According to his draft registration, he lived at Carlton Apartments in Long Beach while working in San Pedro. He received a regular remittance from England, maybe small, but it nevertheless freed him from the immediate worries of making a consistent living.

EDWIN COOPER INTERVIEW

No one knows you better than your postman—your interests, income sources, religious and political affiliation and whether you pay your bills or not. In a March 29, 1972 interview conducted by June Dougherty with Edwin Cooper (the postmaster in La Cañada for twenty-eight years) and his daughter, they discussed Charlie:

> *He was a remittance man all his life. Got remittance from England. Not a very big one. But they took care of him to a certain extent all his life.*

He was a T*ALL very thin man. Boy, he was thinner than I and that is thin enough. For long years he always wore high boots.*

Cooper's daughter—High boots, real high boots. He A*LWAYS wore the same kind of sort of a cowboy hat turned up. Well, it was* A*LWAYS the same style. A felt hat. His wife tried to get him to change his ways, but he didn't change.*

Edwin—Colored shirts. He wasn't a man to dress very much.

Edwin's daughter—You would notice him in a crowd because he was so different. A picture will tell you that right away.

NATURALIZATION

Pate was in no hurry to seek America citizenship; he first submitted a declaration of intent on July 29, 1913, twenty-one years after he had immigrated. He kind of fudged on his declaration, stating that he first came to the United States in 1904, but this was when he returned from the family's yearlong visit to England. He received his citizenship papers on December 24, 1915. His witnesses were Thomas McClellan Hall and J.H. Armstrong.

Why he waited so long is not known; maybe he thought that he might move back to England, or maybe it was to secure automatic citizenship for his minor daughter, Florence. In his naturalization application, Pate stated that he was five feet, eleven inches tell and weighed 145 pounds.

LOSING FAMILY

Mary Wilbur Pate passed away on July 26, 1956, and sadly, Florence passed away suddenly the next year, leaving Charles alone. All of his siblings in England had predeceased him. It is interesting that Florence was engaged to Lloyd Lanterman at the time of her death, as noted by the *Crescenta Valley Ledger* on March 24, 1957:

Florence Pate Sudden Death Shocks Friends

Funeral services were held yesterday morning for Mary Florence Pate, daughter of Charles F. Pate of La Canada. Rites were in the Chapel of Sacred Memories of L.G. Scovern and Son Mortuary, with interment at Forest Lawn.

Miss Pate is survived only by her father, Charles Pate, and by her fiancé, Lloyd Lanterman. She passed away suddenly on Thursday morning, at the family home, 4635 Hillard, on property where her father has lived since 1893.

Miss Pate was born on May 17, 1904 in England, where her parents had gone on an extended visit. She was brought to America when only a few months of age, and the family resumed residence at the Hillard avenue address. Florence Pate was schooled in La Canada and Glendale High School, later studying music in London for two years.

After her return to California, Miss Pate often entertained at local musical gatherings, but entered a business career instead of following her music. For the past 15 years, she had been associated with a florist firm in Los Angeles.

Her mother, Mrs. Mary Pate, passed away last summer, after a prolonged illness. She had been a teacher in La Canada School soon after its founding, a founder of the PTA of La Canada, and served as president of the La Canada Thursday Club.

Florence Pate, daughter of a truly pioneer La Canada family, will be mourned by her many friends.

Charles died on February 20, 1961, at a hospital in Glendale after suffering a fall at his home, as noted by the *La Canada Valley Sun* on February 23, 1961:

Services Today for Pioneer Hillard Resident
Charles F. Pate, La Canadan Since 1893, Dies

Charles Frederick Pate, nearly 87 and one of the first settlers in La Canada—-coming here in 1893, died Monday at Glendale Memorial Hospital, 10 days after he had broken his pelvis in a fall at his home on Hillard Avenue.

Funeral services are scheduled for today at 2 p.m. at the L.G. Scovern & Son Chapel of Sacred Memories, 828 S. Brand Blvd., Glendale. Officiating at the services will be the Rev. Boone Sadler Jr., rector at St. Luke's of the Mountains Episcopal Church in La Crescenta. Interment will probably be at Forest Lawn where members of Mr. Pate's family are buried.

The local man, who would have been 87 on March 7, was one of this community's early pioneers, coming here in 1893, when La Canada's population was a mere handful—150—compared with the current 18,525. In the late 19th and early 20th century, the community was primarily an agricultural area. Few houses could be seen among the miles of fruit orchards and vineyards as well as uncultivated land. Dirt roads and paths bordered the parcels of land in the Crescenta-Canada Valley.

English-Born

Mr. Pate was born in Eltham, England (the same birthplace as comedian Bob Hope), and came to the United States and the West Coast (Glendora) six months before choosing La Canada as his home. His late wife, Mrs. Mary Wilber Pate (who he married in 1897) had once said:

"This was a fellow who had just left an exclusive boys' school in England and had never worked a day in his life before he came to this country."

Mrs. Pate was at one time teacher of grades 1–8 in the two-room wood frame school house where the La Canada Elementary School is now located. She later became president of the charter PTA chapter in La Canada. She passed away about three years ago as did Mr. Pate's daughter, Florence.

Worked for Dr. Lanterman

Upon arrival in La Canada, Mr. Pate was employed as an apricot picker by Dr. Jacob Lanterman, one of the principal landowners and founders of early-day La Canada, on his Homewood (now Verdugo Boulevard) estate. The present site of the Church of the Lighted Window was among the farm land worked then.

With money earned on this job and several other farm jobs, Mr. Pate purchased five acres of land in the old Hillard tract. There, he planted and maintained a grove of peach and French prune trees. Irrigation then was done by piping water from the canyon flow on the mountain slopes. No water companies were in existence at that time.

Sold Most of Land

He built his first home in 1894. During the years, he sold most of his five acres although retaining a parcel where his current residence at 4635 Hillard, built in 1916, is located.

Mr. Pate was engaged in other jobs, too, as he worked for what is now known as the La Canada Irrigation District as a line layer and used his ability as a carpenter to help construct the Church of the Lighted Window. During World War I, he was employed in the shipyards at San Pedro. In World War II, he volunteered and served in the California Highway Patrol Auxiliary.

The local pioneer leaves a niece, Mrs. Dimice Shroyer of Montebello; three nephews, Raymond Wilber of 4621 Orange Knoll Ave., La Canada; Jack Wilber of Glendale and J. Robert Parker of Arcadia; and a sister-in-law, Mrs. Nancy Wilber of Azusa.

THE WILL

Charles F. Pate appointed Willard M. Shroyer, the husband of his niece, Dimice D. Shroyer, as executor of his will. There were three separate disbursements of the estate by 1966, but it was dragged out for many years for no apparent reason. The finalization of the will was not done until ten years after Pate's death, and only after Willard had died and Dimice had replaced him as executor. Dimice Parker Shroyer was the daughter of Mary Wilber Pate's sister, Nellie, who had settled in El Centro, California.

Charles left an estate consisting of $105,739.63 in cash, as well as his residence at 4635 Hillard Avenue, La Cañada, which sold for $32,100. His personal property was assessed at $100.

Dimice and her husband each received $40,000 in cash, and Dimice was left all the furnishings and personal effects. No mention was made of the photographic collection that ended up at the Congregational Church of La Cañada.

He left $8,000 each to nieces Norma Jean and Agnes Wilber and nephew Raymond, as well as to Lloyd L. Lanterman. He left $4,000 each to neighbors Herbert and Ina Uren, Sidney and Katherine Fuller, Willlis and Ruth Freitag and Starr and Mary Barnum.

Number 4635 Hillard Avenue is no longer an address in La Cañada. Charles, Mary and Florence are buried next to each other at Forest Lawn Memorial Park, Glendale, California (right behind the Chandler Monument).

As far as his regular remittance(s) from England, he had several foreign stocks: British Railway Stock; Lester Ryons & Company stock dividends;

Barclays, London–British War Stock Interest; Central Argentine Railway Limited stocks; and other U.S. stock accounts, all of which were listed as assets in his will. There was no mention of a trust in the will, but a 1962 probate court date for him in England is listed in an online database with any further information, so there was some financial issue in England to finalize after his death.

TENDERFOOT

> *"A newcomer in a comparatively rough or newly settled region, especially one not hardened to frontier or outdoor life."*

Charles Pate was an avid photographer; his photo collection is owned by the Congregational Church of La Cañada and is housed at the Lanterman Museum Archives. He wrote a seventy-nine-page uncompleted manuscript, "Reminiscences of a Tenderfoot," that is also housed at the Lanterman Museum Archives. While Pate's writings are an invaluable part of Valley history, he has also contributed to some of the misconceptions about early pioneers, written many years after the fact and many times based on secondhand information. A friend, Ralph Moses, remarked that Pate never allowed facts to get in the way of a good story.

Pate had a romanticized view of his life in the West, far from the sometimes rigid English society in which he was raised; he was not exactly rich, but he was mostly free from the day-to-day struggle to make a living.

In June Dougherty's research material at the Lanterman Archives, she wrote about Pate and his slant on history regarding the schoolhouse dance conflict in 1894. This material was not incorporated into her book *La Crescenta: Sources of History* as it concerned La Cañada, but it was instead used as teaching material for local schoolteachers:

> *After conflict with his Glendora employer he moved to La Canada to work for the Lanterman family. Most of the rest of his life was spent clearing land for ranches, as a fruit grower on his own land, helping to develop the gravity water system, fighting fires and other activities on the farm community. He had few encumbrances. At twenty six in the 1900 census he was listed as unmarried and owner of a farm with no mortgage. He*

Pate and his well-used Model T touring car. *Courtesy of La Cañada Congregational Church photography collection at Lanterman Museum Archives.*

> *was known to be a "remittance man" receiving regular payments from his family in England. He married a young teacher who came to work in La Canada in 1902. Except for two trips to England he spent most of his life in La Canada. He loved to talk and had a "good speaking voice." He loved to hunt, hike and write.*
>
> *His account, written long after the incidents, was not tempered by many years of anxious parenthood of a large family. He had only one child. His story presents the viewpoint of a free young person annoyed by the criticism of elders, elated by their defeat and enjoying the conflict. Pate's attitude toward dancing and the social life of the community reflects his age of twenty years at the time of the incident, his distance from family problems and his not having a frontier family background with its sobering hardships.*

Charles was aware of the fact that some people thought that he had it a little easier than most—he did name his manuscript "Reminiscences of a Tenderfoot" after all. In it, he wrote about the realities of Valley life as he saw them:

> *I am a realist and have been punched in the ribs by a plough-handle when the point hit one of these loved rocks: I have worn the skin off my hands when handling them and, in short, I have found nothing loveable about them. There was no poetry about being out in the pouring rain; gathering wet brush, and tramping it into the winter rills to prevent them from cutting things to pieces.*

While Charles left no descendants, he left extensive writings about the early days, as well as his photograph collection, which has been extensively used in local history publications. He deserves to be remembered.

CHAPTER 9

GOULD CASTLE

A Lost Treasure or an Attractive Nuisance?

Probably no Valley landmark has had more written about it than Gould Castle. In researching the site, going back to the original records and newspaper articles of the day, I have tried to present a new look of what actually transpired.

It was never called Gould Castle by the original owners. They called it "the Castle." It was newspaper reporters and locals who later gave it the present moniker. After the Goulds moved out in 1897, it was renamed "Castle del Crescenta" by the Cohens and remained so for more than thirty years. Most articles in the last sixty years note that the owner and builder was Eugene Gould. Actually, it was his wife, May Isabel Briggs, who designed, oversaw construction, owned and paid for the Castle. In the nineteenth century, a woman could own real estate as her sole and separate property if it was purchased with money that she brought into the marriage. May was the daughter of George Gregg Briggs, the brother of Dr. Benjamin B. Briggs, who founded and developed La Crescenta. George Briggs died in 1885 and left a large estate. May and her sister were raised with great privilege and were not expected to have to improve themselves or to earn a living. When George died, his wife, Emma, hid the will, as she wanted control of the estate. Eventually, all of George's wealth was squandered by his descendants.

May had visited her uncle, Dr. Briggs, in La Crescenta and purchased property from him in 1890, as reported in a notice in the September 25, 1890 *Los Angeles Times*:

The Castle in the early days before the lush landscaping had grown in.

Real-Estate Transfers

BB Briggs to Mrs. Mary J. Gould—All that part of lots 1 and 2 and E½ of NE ¼ of section 27, township 2 north range 13 W. lying on east site of Pickens and Mullally Cañons; also lot 3 in SE¼ of section 27, township 2 north, range 13 west, also E½ of SW ¼ of NW ¼ of section 26, township 2 north, range 13 west and water, also right-of-way over W ½ of NW¼ of section 26, township 2 north, range 13 west, $12,000.

The deed for the sale of the Castle land was recorded on July 2, 1890, at the Los Angeles County Recorder's Office (Book 678). The deed presents a good picture of the parties involved. The land was not part of Dr. Briggs's original purchase of land from J.L. Lanterman that became the basis of present-day La Crescenta, but rather it came from other land transactions that had been made by Dr. Briggs. The Castle was located in La Cañada and was above the Rancho La Cañada border and included railroad land that Briggs had purchased from Lanterman. It is interesting that May Gould was not around to sign the original deed, but she did come into the recorder's office two months later to obtain a copy:

This Indenture made the second day of July in the year of our Lord one thousand eight hundred and ninety.

Between B.B. Briggs of Los Angeles County, State of California, the party of the first part and Mrs. May J. Gould of San Francisco, the same state, party of the second part.

Witnesseth that the said party of the first part for and in consideration of the sum of twelve thousand ($12,000.00) dollars lawful money of the United States of America, to him in hand paid by the said party of the second part, the receipt whereof is hereby acknowledged, has granted, bargained and sold, conveyed and confirmed, and by these presents, does grant, bargain and sell, convey and confirm, unto the said party of the second part, and to her heirs and assigns forever, all those certain lots, pieces or parcels of land situate lying and being in the County of Los Angeles, State of California and bounded and particularly described as follows, to wit: Being all of that portion of Lots 1 & 2 and the E ½ of the N.E. ¼ of section No. 27 in Township 2 North of Range 13 West S.B.M. lying upon the east side of the Pickens and Mullaly Canons containing about 95 acres of land more or less also all those certain lots, pieces or parcels of land, bounded and described as follows, to wit. Lot 3 in the S.E. ¼ of Section 27 Township 2 N, Rg. 13 W. S.B.M. containing 37 47/100 acres of land more or less and being the same land conveyed to A.J. Lanterman by the Southern Pacific Rail Road Company by deed dated Oct. 23 A.D. 1880 recorded in Book 103 page 150 of Recorders of Los Angeles County, also the easterly ½ of the S.W. ¼ of the N.W. ¼ of Section 26, Township 2 N. Re. 13 W. S.B.M. The two last above described tracts of land containing in all 57 47/100 acres of land.

This deed is also extended to convey to section parties all of the waters flowing from two springs on the right hand or easterly branch of the Snover Cañon and all of the water arising on said easterly branch above a point where said Snover Cañon forks a little to the East of Snover Cañon and also the right of way over the W. ½ of the N.W. ¼ of Section 26, T. 2 N., Rg. 13 W. S.B.M. to the lands of the above parcels of the first. Reserving to A.J. Lanterman and J.L. Lanterman the right to construct and box in the wash from what is known as Snover Cañon somewhere on the N.W. corner of the same above described tract or on the S.W. corner of the lands of the parties of the first part adjoining.

Together with all and singular the comments herestaments and appurtenances thereunto belonging or in anywhere appertaining and the reversions and reversions, remainder and remainders, rents, issues and profits hereof.

To Have and to Hold, all and singular, the said premises, together with the appurtenances unto the said party of the second part, her heirs and assigns forever. The property is bought with her separate money coming from the estate of her father.

In Witness. Whereof the said party of the first part, has hereunto set his hand and seal the day and year first above written.

(Signed, Sealed and Delivered in the Presence of) B.B. Briggs
(State of California)
(County of Los Angeles)

On the 2nd day of July in the year one thousand eight hundred and ninety before me, Jas. S. MacKenzie, a Notary Public in and for said County residing therein, duly commissioned and sworn, personally appeared B.B. Briggs known to me to be the person described in and whose name is subscribed to the within instrument and acknowledged to me that he executed the same.

A full true and correct copy of the original recorded at request of Grantee Sept. 28, 1890 at 25 min. past 10 A.M.

John W, Francis, County Recorder.

Construction began in the spring of 1891, according to the May 22, 1891 *Los Angeles Herald*:

Mrs. Eugene Gould's place is at present the scene of more activity than any other one place in our valley. A beautiful and commodious house, worthy to crown this commanding height, is to be built at once, the grading for which is going on rapidly. The house will be of stone and concrete, using the beautiful granite of this place, and is planned with special reference to the climate and location. An immense reservoir over fifty feet square is being built, of solid concrete, which will be as strong as the everlasting hills and almost as enduring.

Quite a bit of engineering has been accomplished there. It is a cable track from the bed of the creek, hundreds of feet below, to the site of the house to be built, and to the reservoir. On this track runs a car carrying over a ton at a load, which transports the stone and sand to the point where they are used. This is operated by a horse.

The reservoir, essential for living in the foothills in the nineteenth century.

Once it was nearing completion, the November 18, 1891 *Los Angeles Herald* gave an update on the site:

> *Mrs. Eugene Gould's beautiful residence upon the mountain side is progressing toward completion, and they hope to occupy it before the winter is over. It is one of the attractions of this locality, and makes considerable business for the Glendale branch of the Terminal railroad, as all the materials—except that found upon the place, is brought by the road to Verdugo park, and from thence by wagon. Over 100 barrels of cement alone are used in the construction, and other material in proportion.*

Above: Arches at the Castle.

Left: View from the roof of the castle looking east.

Excerpts from an article written by Mike Lawler in the December 29, 2011 *Crescenta Valley Weekly* give a good picture of the Castle structure:

> *The land was just to the east across Pickens Canyon, near what is today the top of Ocean View, and a 185 acre estate was envisioned by May Gould with a stone castle as its centerpiece.*
>
> *May drew up the concept for the castle and local rancher Charles Bathey who lived in nearby Goss Canyon was hired as foreman for this amazing construction feat. It wouldn't be made of rough alluvial rock, but the more elegant cut stone.*
>
> *The granite blocks for the thick walls were to be quarried from the thousands of boulders strewn about the valley floor. The stones were cut wherever they were found, and with no power tools available, ancient methods were employed. The natural fissures in the massive boulders were observed, and small holes were hand-drilled or chipped at the fissure's heads. From there, small "feathers" or wooden wedges were hammered in to carefully crack the stones into workable blocks.*
>
> *The grounds of the estate were terraced with miles of rock walls, and rare shrubs and trees were planted on the various levels. Expansive orchards of citrus and olive trees were planted and an elaborate irrigation system of pipes was installed, fed by a 60- by 60-foot reservoir that tapped into mountain springs.*
>
> *In 1892, the castle was completed. The west wing contained the living quarters, bedrooms, and a tall tower that held May's studio. The east wing had an impressive main hall, framed with marble columns and arched windows, plus a big dining room, kitchens and cellars. The two wings of the massive structure were separated by a courtyard containing rare plants and a huge koi pond, surrounded by castellated walls and a wide veranda that ran along the front.*

Various accounts have the Castle being Moorish in style and based on medieval castles that May saw in Algiers or Spain. A 1906 article in a design magazine noted the style as Andalusian, which is Spanish. By the time it was torn down, it had toilets and showers—whether these were original to the structure is not known, but it did have a fifty-foot-square reservoir for domestic needs. The servants' quarters were under the main building. The family lived on a cottage on the property until the Castle was finished; this undoubtedly became the caretaker's house.

After construction was completed, the Goulds went up north for a six-month sojourn, according to the June 19, 1892 *Los Angeles Herald*: "Mr.

May Gould, with the children on roof. Was she yelling at them to get down? *Courtesy of Lori Ward Kent.*

Eugene Gould and family leave their beautiful home in Crescenta this week for Oakland, where they expect to stay until next December."

After they returned in December, it is doubtful that Eugene Gould could have conducted his business activities from such a remote location—there was no telephone and such. He had an office in Los Angeles, and he would not have commuted back and forth from Los Angeles every day. Eugene is never in family pictures at the Castle. After they moved out permanently in December 1897, the Castle was never occupied on a full-time basis again; there were sporadic caretakers hired, but the property was vacant at times. This led to constant vandalism and deterioration of the Castle property. It was a popular place for people to visit, picnic and take pictures, all while ignoring the "No Trespassing/Shoot Anyone Entering" signs.

CHARLES BATHEY

No Valley resident was more connected to the Castle than Charles Bathey. He came to the Valley in 1882 and supported his wife and five children by

ELEVATION 2200 FEET SCENERY UNSURPASSED

The Castle del Crescenta.

A DELIGHTFUL AND PICTURESQUE BOARDING PLACE

PERFECT VIEW OF THE VALLEY, OCEAN AND CATALINA

Fourteen Miles from Los Angeles. Five Miles from Verdugo Park.

TERMS REASONABLE

Conveyances may be ordered to connect with trains at Verdugo Park by giving two days notice.

Address C. T. BATHEY,

OVER *LA CRESCENTA, LOS ANGELES CO., CAL.*

Charles Bathey postcard advertising the Castle for rent.

farming and construction work. Originally a dairyman in Los Angeles, he was the foreman on the building of the Castle and was involved on and off with its operation for many years. When the Castle was being built, May insisted on laying the wood floors on bare dirt, with no foundation or floor vents, despite Bathey's pleas not to do so. The floors rotted within a few years and were ripped up, leaving dirt floors.

Around 1896, Bathey and his wife were renting the Castle property; the exact situation is not known. The Batheys lived in the caretaker's cottage for about a year. This did not work out, and May Gould had to sue Charles Bathey and his wife, Mary, in court to get them to move out, according to the January 16, 1897 *Los Angeles Times*:

> *Agreed to Move—An agreement was reached in the case of May I. Gould, owner of the La Crescenta Castle against C.T. Bathey and wife, lessees of the building. It was an action for rent and recovery of premises tried before Justice Young. The defendants agreed to surrender the property, the plaintiff called it square.*

After the Goulds left, Charles again acted as a caretaker and was in charge of renting out the property, now called Castle del Crescenta. By 1910, Mary Bathey had died, and Charles and the children were now living in Los Angeles; their La Crescenta ranch became a second home.

LOST FORTUNE

There have been several different theories presented about how the Goulds lost their fortune. May Gould inherited part of a large estate from her father, George Gregg Briggs, reportedly the first millionaire in the state of California, coming here in 1849. She married Eugene Gould, a superintendent on her father's raisin farm, around 1882. Eugene has been referred to as a ranch hand, but in actuality, he was from a very successful farm family. In the 1860 census, his father reported a $75,000 net worth, a fortune at that time. Eugene has also been called a "raisin king," but it was actually his father-in-law, George Briggs, who was the raisin king. When George came to California in 1849, instead of heading to the gold fields, he made a fortune by providing fresh melons and other fruit crops to the exploding population.

As May was not raised to work, was never expected to work and had always been taken care of by her father, she undoubtedly turned the business aspects of the marriage over to her husband. They purchased several properties around the state, all with mortgages, three obtained from Mrs. Emelie Cohen. It has been said that Eugene Gould lost his fortune by trying to corner the raisin market, but a raisin cooperative was established in the 1880s in California that controlled prices among the members. A family history written by Dr. Briggs's descendant, Irene Ward Kennedy, stated that Eugene tried to corner the wheat market and lost his fortune.

While they were still living in the Castle, Eugene became involved in gold mining in Randsburg, Kern County, California. A February 1898 newspaper article referred to Eugene having "mining interests in Randsburg and judging from the present showing of the St. Elmo mine, he will have in a few years the mythical fortune referred to transmuted into a tangible reality."

The loss of May's inheritance was most likely a combination of having too many properties with mortgages on them, a lavish lifestyle and several different speculative ventures, and eventually everything came down like a house of cards.

Edgar Cohen, Scapegoat

Edgar A. Cohen was never the mortgagee or owner of Gould Castle. His mother, Emelie Cohen, was the person who carried the mortgages for May I. Gould. When Emelie's husband, Alfred, died in 1887, he left his large fortune, properties and assets to her—nothing to any of their children. Emelie hired her sons to help run the Cohen enterprises. She named her son Edgar trustee of the Gould mortgages. When the Goulds did not pay the notes when they came due in January 1896, Edgar was supposed to foreclose on it; he did not do so, and his mother sued to remove him as trustee. Edgar has been sometimes portrayed as a villain in the foreclosure of the Castle, but the following article from the December 18, 1897 *Los Angeles Herald* shows that he was reluctant and that it was his mother, the holder of the mortgages, who authorized the foreclosures. The mortgages were taken out a year after the Castle was completed:

> *A Receiver Removed*
> *On Application of a Heavy Creditor*
> *Land Must Be Sold to Provide for the Payment of the Gould Loan*
>
> *San Francisco, Dec. 17—The London and San Francisco bank was today given judgment b Judge Morrow of the United States circuit court in its suit to have Edgar A. Cohen of Alameda removed as trustee of considerable property in the state.*
>
> *The litigation arose out of the loan of $70,500 made by Mrs. Emilie Cohen, his mother, in 1893, to May Gould and her husband, Eugene H. Gould.*
>
> *To secure the loan three notes were given by Mrs. Gould and her husband, each for 23,500. And a trust deed to property situated in various parts of the state was executed, of which deed Edgar A. Cohen was made trustee. The deed provided that in the event of the notes not being paid, the trustee should be empowered to sell any or all of the real estate at the demand of the holder of the notes.*
>
> *Mrs. Cohn, shortly after the notes came into her possession, assigned them to the London and San Francisco bank.*
>
> *In January 1896, two of the notes fell due, and the bank, as holder of them, called upon Mrs. Gould and her husband to pay them. They failed to do so, and the bank then notified Edgar A. Cohen to sell the real estate of the Goulds' of which he was trustee. He failed to do this, though repeatedly requested by the bank to do so, hence this suit.*

The Gould children—Winston, Theodore and Dorothy—all dressed up, circa 1895.

> *Judge Morrow this morning gave judgment in favor of the bank and removed Cohen from his trusteeship.*
>
> *His successor will be appointed in a few days, and the real estate, which is situated in San Francisco, Oakland, Alameda, Fresno and Los Angeles, will be sold under the terms of the deed of trust, as prayed for by the bank.*

Two months before the foreclosure order, what appears to be an act of desperation on the part of May and probably Eugene was to declare Eugene dead so that May could collect his life insurance. He, of course, was not dead. What this was about is anyone's guess, as noted here by the *Los Angeles Times* from October 18, 1897:

> *New Suits Filed*
>
> *Matter of the estate and guardianship of Winston Eugene Gould, Theodore Gould and Dorothy Marguerite Gould—Petition by their mother, May I. Gould to be appointed their guardian for the proper care of the children's interest in a policy of life insurance of Eugene H. Gould, their deceased father.*

There were many problems with the property—water rights, property disputes and fires over the thirty-plus years that the Cohens owned the property—and clearing the title took many years. They put a caretaker on the property, but several newspaper articles reported on the extensive vandalism of the Castle. Various members of the Gould family would visit. Edgar Cohen by this time had started to devote his time to photography and took many photographs of the Castle.

EUGENE AND MAY GOULD

It has been reported that after they left the Castle in 1897, Eugene and May moved back up north, but they actually stayed in Southern California. In the 1900 census, May and her three children—Winston, Theodore and Dorothy—were living in Santa Monica, and she was listed as divorced. Eugene cannot be found in this census. In 1910, May and Eugene were living in Burbank, married, and Eugene listed his occupation as a gold miner. In 1920, May and Eugene were living in San Luis Obispo, and he was a storekeeper for an oil company. Eugene died in September 1929 and May a year later, in August 1930. They are both buried at Forest Lawn Memorial Park in Glendale, California. Gould Avenue in La Cañada was not named for them but rather for Will D. Gould, a prominent Los Angeles attorney who owned a large property at the top of Gould Avenue as a secondary residence.

The Castle was an adolescent dream of an impractical woman, expensive and difficult to maintain. It was remote; anyone who could afford to buy and maintain it would have had to have a huge personal fortune and/or live in Los Angeles to work to support it. It was always a secondary property for subsequent owners. The grounds were at times well maintained and were used for daytime social events, and it has been reported that horror movies were sometimes filmed there. It had been periodically vandalized since 1898, and by the time it was torn down, it had been stripped of all its original furniture and fixtures. Even on its best day, it was a nice place to visit, but would you really want to live there?

The property was located in La Cañada at what was then the top of Ocean View (originally Main Street); however, Ocean View has been extended over the years and goes higher up the hill. The Castle site is located between Canalda Drive and Fairhurst Drive off Ocean View. At the end of

Canalda, look left and up, and you are looking at where it was located. For another view, drive to end of Fairhurst (a private road) and look right. You cannot actually see the lot as it is higher and obscured by trees; if you want to view the site, you have to hike up there from Fairhurst—a steep hike up a ravine, no less. A large Italian Stone Pine that was right next to the Castle still stands. A Google map search will show a large, empty lot between the ends of Canalda and Fairhurst. No foundations remain, but there are several large "cut" stones around the lot.

The following two articles were written after the Goulds moved out and while the Castle was still in reasonably good shape; they were written in the flowery style of day. The first article notes that the Castle had electricity, but that did not come to the Valley until 1911, and all the early pictures show no sign of electrical wires.

The House Beautiful, vol. VII, no. I, December 1899
Del Crescenta—A California Chateau

"The queen o' fairies, she caught me,
In this green hill to dwell."

It is an enchanted land, and even plain, hard-headed business men yield to its spell, and become captives of the Circe who dwells in these purple hills.

Who would imagine this to be an American home, built in the last years of the hustling, driving nineteenth century, in practical, realistic, machine-making Yankeedom, the land of the skyscraper and the "modern flat"! Is it not a veritable "Chateau en Espagne," and would you not swear those were the blue hills of the Pyrenees! Surely the forests of Vallambrosa are nearby, and the golden grapes of Valencia are sweetening under that cloudless sky.

One can smell the oleanders and the palm-gardens of Elche in that soft and odorous air, hear the tinkle of guitars, and see the velvet bodice and bright-colored manta of the Moorish main glancing through those arches. At any rate, no Castilian castle could well wear a more romantic aspect or be placed in a more picturesque setting than this California home in the foothills of the Sierra Madre, near Pasadena. For the half circle—crescent-shaped, as its name implies—of stone arches and central tower, the gray granite of the hills affords a construction to last forever, and one that well suits the romantic style of the architecture.

The massive outlines of the Moorish tower, the arches of the colonnade, the deep embrasures of the windows, the embattle parapets of the walls,

Tower and back steps to May Gould's studio. *Courtesy Glendale Public Library Special Collections.*

the patio, with its vine-draped plaster sides, the deeply recessed stone loggia, opening upon the walled terraces below—all are interesting features, and form an ensemble worthy to be placed under the blue shadows, awesome and mysterious, of the Sierra Madre. The wooded slopes and rugged canon the nearer foothills are just at the door, while in the distance show faintly in dim outline vista after vista of the range itself, from whose snow-fed springs is piped the water to make the rose-gardens and fountains of terrace and court.

The view from this terrace of smiling vineyards and the rich gloom of grange-groves in the vega below is magnificent, while from the parapet above one can see in that luminous atmosphere where, thirty miles away, shimmers the white shining line of the sea.

As we pass up the broad flights of steps into the vestibule, we note that the arched doorways and windows are ornamented with wrought iron in arabesque designs.

Mingled lights and shadows move over the mosaic of the pavement. The interior woodwork is mostly of cedar, with vaulted and beamed ceilings.

Though seven miles into the foothills, the dwelling is fitted up with every modern convenience in electricity and plumbing. The crystal candelabra, the yellow ivory of the walls, with arabesque decorations in gold, carry out

Castle arches and steps.

the Moorish idea, while a profusion of tropical fruits and flowers adds to the foreign air.

Nor could any Andalusian garden boast greater wealth of olive and palm. About the stone pillars of the portal the bignonia-vine hangs its brilliant orange-colored clusters of trumpet-shaped bloom in wreaths and garlands. Ivy and rose vines mingle their greenery in riotous profusion around the arches of the loggia. A wealth of heliotrope—that lover of the sun—against the stone steps makes the air heavy with sweetness.

Gorgeous lilies of the crimson hibiscus vie with the flaming poinsettia in the sheltered angles, masses of glowing color against the gray stone.

The scarlet tassels of the mountain sage nod along the walls of the terraces, and a La Marque rose, with a trunk like a tree, covers the entrance-gate with white bloom.

Here in this land of the sun, where "a' the sweets o' spring and summer grow," where the flowers of earth "vie with the stars of heaven," asking only a cup of water when they faint in the too fierce rays of that intense sunshine, it is possible to have all these things. It is possible, too, to live largely in the court, upon which open the doors of living and dining room, and of sleeping rooms as well. What a charming spot to open a casement window upon in the dew and freshness of a California morning! Or to lean out and pluck a rose that the breeze swings in and out. What a delicious flavor is added to the morning Mocha as that flower-laden air sweeps lightly through the open door.

Here you may draw the light sewing chair, while the needle flashes in the sun and the dainty stitches grow and grow in this delightful open-air sewing room.

Here one may pass dreamy, languorous hours, lulled by the splashing of the fountain as it cooling spray tempers the heat. Here the Virginia creeper clings to the gray plaster of the wall in a delicate lace-like web, and the plumbago covers one corner with its blue blossoms. The bougainvillea, purple and proud, and dreaming still of the stuccoed balcony of Algiers, when it was torn to grace these western walls, trails across another corner, while beds of rare flowers and tropical plants are placed about the paved court in the angles and intersections.

It is pathetic to think that this beautiful southern home has passed, through money losses, out of the ownership of the man who had the artistic I imagination to build it and to place it in such an environment into the hands of strangers. More pathetic still, that all this bloom and beauty is slowly withering and dying while one of those endless California litigations as to the water-rights drags it slow length through the courts.

The fountain's cooling spray no longer flashes in the sunlight, nor do the birds drink from the edge of the basin. The roses hang their lovely heads and brambles choke the flower beds. Silence reigns in the courtyard where once was laughter and gay song.

The caretaker who showed us the lovely place, and furnished us with water for our picnic coffeepot, had brought the water half a mile in a bucket. The wheel was broken at the cistern and the faucets were dry. All this because another had tunneled behind this house-holder, back in the hills, and drawn off his water into another channel.

Truly one may well feel a little shy of this "garden spot of the world" where such things be, where you may wake up some fine morning with no water to make your coffee.

A long and expensive litigation is now vexing the souls of the owners of this lovely chateau, and if finally successful, much time and money will be required to restore it to its first beauty.

Henrietta Jewett.

The International Studio
An Illustrated Magazine of Fine And Applied Art
Volumes 32–33
Comprising July, August, September and October 1907
Numbers 125 to 128
The California Patio by Henrietta Keith
Two Types of the California Patio

Of the many beautiful patios in California, the court of what is known as "Gould Castle," some eight miles back in the Sierra Madre foothills from Pasadena, is perhaps the most typically Andalusian in character.

The frowning gray walls of this massive stone castle against its mountain setting might, in truth, have belonged to some mediaeval castle of old Granada itself, transplanted by an Afrite's magic from their native fastnesses and dropped into this new world setting.

A superb promenade crowns the castle wall, from whence one looks forth upon the snow-capped tops of the Sierra peaks; nearer are the purpled hills, and nearer yet gray olive orchards, the black plumes of cypress hedges and sunny gardens.

All the living and sleeping-rooms of the house give upon the inner court or patio, through irregularly placed openings on three sides, who charm is seen in the photographs. Neither pictures nor words, however, can convey the beauty of the laced-like decorations of iron crowning these, or the still more delicate leafage and tendril of the clinging vines—against the solid gray walls. This contrast of delicate grace and massive strength is further emphasized in the heavy-barred oaken doors, with iron hinges nailed across. Wrought iron lamps swing in corners, from long, slender wrought iron brackets.

THE PASSING OF AN ERA

The Castle's last days were in October 1955. Sold to developers, it was demolished by a local contractor, Rakisits Engineering; the granite stones were dumped in the ravine to the east. Joe Rakisits was a young man and worked on the demolishing and grading and had also hung out there with friends when he was a teenager. He shared his memories of the Castle and remembered that the roof was green, which means that it was copper and not lead or tar paper, as has been reported. The grounds and landscaping were in very good condition, but the Castle buildings had been vandalized and gutted of everything of value. The roads were not paved at that time, and the property was graded for development.

It was a different time; the postwar 1950s was a time of the baby boomer generation and the suburban housing development explosion, when an average person could at last achieve the American dream of owning their own single-family dwelling. People then were not concerned with historical preservation; there was no hue and cry, no letters to the editor or editorials lamenting the loss of the Castle. No one fell in love with it or had the deep pockets to restore it one more time, so it went quietly.

The Castle right before it was torn down, with the landscaping removed.

Grace and Arthur Carpenter and their three boys were caretakers at the Castle for two years when they came to California in 1920, before they helped establish the local *Ledger* newspaper. They stayed in the ranch house, which was located a distance away next to the barn. Grace wrote about a last visit to the Castle in the October 13, 1955 *Ledger* paper, but oddly, she speaks of herself in the third person. In 1955, only her son Don was still living, so this was obviously a very emotional journey. She went with Don and two grandchildren. The landscaping had been removed. Demolition started a week later:

> *Memories Rekindled in Last Visit to Old Gould Castle in Foothills*
> *By Grace Marion Carpenter*
>
> *Stark and unadorned, the old Gould Castle stood proudly against the foothills of the Sierras for a few days last week. Then it bowed its turreted head to the march of progress. Without its screen of venerable trees, the castle appeared as it had looked about 65 years ago when it was first built. At completion its furnishings were sumptuous and the servants many.*
>
> *The castle was the most romantic place in this area and many motion pictures had been made in its gardens. Tally-hos from Pasadena had brought tourists to view its charms, as it was listed in guide books of the Nineties. Its possession had been in argued in San Francisco courts. Then came neglect as the northern owners cared not. After a score of years, it was again prized and blossomed forth.*
>
> *Thirty-five years ago, a father, mother and three small sons found this estate a haven after having spent three months camping across a continent. Although it had no conveniences, it did have a good roof to shelter against rainfall. The castle itself was a shell where tarantulas, centipedes and rattlesnakes lingered, but even the Garden of Eden had its serpent. The ranch house was commodious with a long, wide porch from which the view was unrivaled. The children could clearly count the houses in the Valley—it was no task.*
>
> *The sign at the entrance of the estate, 6/10 of a mile away, was lettered "No Trespassing" which Californians interpreted as "Welcome." The San Francisco owners added: "Shoot anyone entering." The estate had its own water supply and three tunnels in the hills came crystal water.*
>
> *The ranch house was destroyed by fire about 25 years ago. Otherwise, the estate remained intact.*

To pay a farewell visit to a beloved past, the mother, remaining son and two grandchildren made a visit to the estate on Saturday. With red eyes the site was viewed for giant trees had been uprooted locating a magnificent Mt. Atlas Blue Cedar. They had shielded the old building and screened its front. Gone were the stone walls flanking the terraces once gay with flowers. The vines climbed tight against the tower, used by the first mistress as a studio, as if to protect the old globe edifice.

Among the first places viewed was the large pool, no longer clear, where the son guides on Saturday, had been host at a party for La Canada school celebrating the climax of eight years there. The principal, coach and teacher were the special guests. Swimming was the diversion.

The two grandchildren, Kathy and Steve, liked the old barn where the horses, Molly and Dolly, had been stalled, and its adjacent corral. They wished, they too, could have plunged headlong into the new mowed hay heaped in the loft. The hay had been planted and harvested by the father, a city man, in the vast fields that stretched eastward to the pink Strong's Castle. They were told how the mice came to nibble the grain and how the boys were paid two cents apiece for the rodents caught. The fund was used to buy Burgress books.

Kathy and Steve stood on the east rim of Pickens Canyon and looked down on the place where the youngest boy had fallen. Across the canyon and through the dense greasewood on the west side, Dick, the oldest boy and for a while Don, his brother, had made their own path to Briggs avenue. They walked the long distances to La Crescenta School, before they entered La Canada.

The grandchildren were intrigued at the Moorish features in several Castle rooms that recalled the fact that Mrs. Eugene Gould, builder, had said it was modeled after one in Algiers. They found the secret closet where one could hide and instantly wanted to see the dungeons! Could the store rooms, jelly cupboards, servants quarters underneath the main house be so called? The laughter of Kathy and Steve while in the spacious courtyard and under the arches of the grand veranda, was of the same gay tone as the laughter of the long ago trio.

There were remnants of the two old olive groves, one in front and the other back of the castle, the peach orchard had disappeared. Dick, Dan and Bob had their favorite trees. Bob's was an acacia, just his height.

As the days drew near to Christmas and the Christ Child was the leading figure in the evening storytelling hour, the mother was startled one day to hear the youngest say, as he hugged the tree, "Little tree, who will

The Gould children with their pony, circa 1896. *Courtesy of Lori Ward Kent.*

Demolishing the Castle in October 1955—the end of an era.

> *get to heaven first, you for me. Soon the site will be smoothed over with the debris deep in the adjacent canyon. Will the wrecking hammers hit both the stone and a Mother's heart. It will mean the end of a daydream, the passing of an era. In a brief time there will be no evidence that a grey stone castle once watched over the valley.*

The Castle itself was torn down for seemingly no good reason; nothing was ever built on the actual site, even though the lot is flat and very large. There may originally have been intentions to build on the site that did not come to pass, or perhaps the contractor did not want to deal with the liability of such a structure, a magnet for vandalism and bored teenagers.

Today, people in Crescenta Valley are constantly fighting to preserve land and historical properties, and it is an expensive, dragged-out process. Sometimes there is success, but who would have the deep pockets even today to maintain this property? While it is certainly a lost treasure, it was also a very attractive (and expensive) nuisance as well.

CHAPTER 10

PROMOTING LA CAÑADA

After Jacob L. Lanterman and Adolphus Wesley Williams purchased the 5,745-acre Ranch La Cañada from Glassell and Chapman in December 1875 for $10,000, they had to start surveying, obtain a stable water supply and develop their property in order to start selling plots of land. The purchase had payment terms, and it took longer to obtain water and develop their property than they originally expected. The final payment deadline was approaching, and a lawsuit and appeal ensued between Lanterman and Williams. They ended up splitting the property into alternate lots running along Michigan Avenue (now Foothill Boulevard).

Jacob's son, Frank, surveyed the property and ended up with a real estate career selling La Cañada land—not only the Lanterman rancho land but also excess school and railroad land. His real estate office was located at the Allen Block on the corner of Temple and Spring Streets in Los Angeles. A promotional flyer from the 1890s gives a rather rosy but informative view of the La Cañada Valley and vigorously promoted it as a health destination:

> *This Delightful Settlement, La Cañada, is located in that almost mountain-bound valley of the same name. It is directly north of Los Angeles and distant about ten miles by the usual traveled road, and lies at the foot of the Sierra Madre Mountains, which bound the valley on the north. With the Verdugo mountains for the southern boundary, and a low range of hills on the western side, the valley may almost be said to be a separate country.*

La Cañada in 1888. *Courtesy of La Cañada Congregational Church photography collection at Lanterman Museum Archives.*

The eastern end, however, is divided from the San Gabriel Valley only by the rocky bed of the Arroyo Seco, which, at this place, is only a few rods wide. Two and one-half miles from here, in a south-easterly direction, lies that pride of Southern California, Pasadena, in all its semi-tropic beauty, being in full view from most points of La Cañada. As the name indicates, the valley is a large, broad cañon, being about two miles in width and some four miles long, containing about five thousand acres, almost all of which is choice land, lying as it does in the far-famed Sierra Madre Slope fruit belt. The land gently slopes to the south-east to within a few rods of the foot of the Verdugo range. The altitude of the valley at the town site is about 1400 feet about the level of the sea, or nearly 1100 feet about the city of Los Angeles, while the portions closer to the mountains on the north reach the altitude of 2000 feet.

SOIL

The soil is of almost every grade and description, It is of a loose, sandy nature at the summit of the valley and increases in richness with great rapidity as you cross the valley from the north to the south, being of a heavy, loamy nature near the Verdugo side. Strata of reddish clayey soil, varying from one-eighth to one-quarter of a mile in width cross the valley from mountain to mountain at intervals of about one or one and one-half miles protecting it from any great danger from washes, and forming natural reservoirs thereby saving the rainfall which insures a good crop of hay even in the driest season by those who properly till the land. These strata are of inexhaustible fertility, producing the best of grape and cherries in abundance. Pears and other fruits requiring heavy land to yield well can here be raised inferior to none.

The most of the land is, however, of that rich alluvial deposit to which Southern California is so largely indebted for its famous fruits and cereals. The great depth of the soil makes it inexhaustible. It has been formed by the slow process of the deposition of the surrounding hills and mountains by the rains of the ages since the world became, and it is therefore of such excellence that it can not be rivaled by any. Alkali, that curse of so many beautiful spots in California, can not be found in the soil, or in the water of the La Cañada Valley, because there is absolutely none there.

Water

The Valley is supplied with water for irrigating and household purposes by mountain springs and streams which rise in the Sierra Madre mountains in great numbers, and furnish pure water in abundance. The waters from these streams and springs are piped on the land they are intended to supply, and with they will be sold, in either iron or cement. The main stream comes what is known as the Pickens Cañon and is carried to the land through 17,000 feet of pipe. This at present delivers on the land about 8,000 barrels of water per day. Another line of pipe conveying a stream of some 2,000 barrels per day, and others of smaller capacity, empty their water on various tracts of land throughout the valley. There can be over 20,000 barrels of water per day thrown onto the portion of land which will be furnished, amounting to some 1,500 acres in all. Other portions of the valley which have not running water can easily be furnished with water for domestic use and for limited irrigation by wells which are obtained at from 50 to 100 feet. The valley is, however, so generally moist that no irrigation is required for grapes or deciduous fruits. None of the water is stored in reservoirs, but comes directly to the consumer's premises, thereby avoiding all stagnation and filth which is unavoidable in an open reservoir. The

The La Cañada school in the late nineteenth century. *Courtesy of La Cañada Congregational Church photography collection at Lanterman Museum Archives.*

water is pure as crystal and free from all alkali or other detrimental matter, and is in such great abundance that it justifies the proprietors in claiming to have the best watered body of highland in Los Angeles county. A certain proportion of the water and water mains is sold with each acre of land, but more can be had if desired by the purchaser at very low prices. This manner of furnishing water to colonies is, it is believed, the best in vogue at present, making each land-owner directly interested in the water and giving him a voice in its management. The direct management, however, falls upon a board of directors who are elected by the water owners, whose duty it is to look after the interests of the community in all water matters.

This is no experimental settlement, but one in which large quantities of all kinds of fruit are raised and have been for years. "Homewood, " the largest improved place in the settlement, consists of a hundred acres, seventy of which are in fruit, vines and trees. Here raisins have been made which San Francisco merchants pronounce the finest they ever handled. Here oranges and lemons of the finest kinds hang thickly on the trees, and apple, pear, peach and apricot trees bear abundantly. This valley is the only place in Southern California where cherry trees bear paying crops, the trees hanging loaded, year after year, to the great surprise of those who always contended that the cherry would not thrive and bear in the southern part of this state. Here, along the mountains, you can raise bananas and other like fruits without the hot-house; in fact no temperate or semi-tropic fruit that has been tried here has failed to reward the grower with fruit. The natural advantages of the valley have crossed every national effort in the fruit-raising line with success.

The settlement now consists of some twenty homes, which together with the crops of the Mexican laborers, give shelter to about one hundred and twenty-five inhabitants; a post-office with a tri-weekly mail, a grocery and novelty store, and a school-house with some twenty pupils enrolled, are among the advantages here offered.

Rainfall

The rain-fall for the slope of the mountains is always more than that for a corresponding length of time in the large valleys farther away. On the Cañada Slope, or in the Cañada Valley, as it may be designated from its position between the hills, the rain-fall always averages one-quarter to one-third more than is recorded in Los Angeles; and from the fact that for the past ten years, since the first settlement there by Americans, they hay and grain crop has always been good, while farther away from the mountains in some years nothing at all was harvested. It may be seen that there is here no fear of a drought, and notwithstanding the amount of water that falls there is never any mind, the roads being just as nice and hard after a rain as they were before.

Not the least attractive part of this settlement is in the scenery, which, from many places in the valley is simply sublime. A fair idea of the view from one of the points may be obtained from the following extract from a letter from the pen of a young gentleman who took a ride out through the Verdugo not long since.

"As we passed along through the canon we were charmed by the romantic scenery. The view of the Cañada slope in front, the high hills on either side, up which steep trails lead to the summits of the peaks. The adobe and reed houses of the Mexicans, the little patches of tilled ground, and the sparkling brook by the road-side were enough to enchant us and prepare as for what was to come the higher we climbed. But for all, we were little prepared for the panorama that was spread before us when we reached the summit of the little hill to which we had unconsciously climbed. There before us nestle the beautiful settlement of La Cañada, with its live oak groves, its vineyards and orange orchards, the patches of newly cleared land, and acres of green underbrush were nothing to mar the scene.

The 1893 Arroyo Seco bridge that made travel to Pasadena much easier. *Courtesy of La Cañada Congregational Church photography collection at Lanterman Museum Archives.*

"Far to the East, was hundred miles distant, rises the rugged peak of San Jacinto, the outline and face of the mountains being as plainly visible as though but a few miles distant, while nearer to us, the upper and central portions of the San Gabriel Valley are in full view. Pasadena and the neighboring settlements show their beauty, while behind us lays the Verdugo Cañon, with the western suburbs of Los Angeles also in view. Farther on Florence and Compton are visible, while the Palos Verdes hills thirty miles distant, with Wilmington and San Pedro lying at the eastern extremity, mark the shore of the ocean, which spreads its glistening waters far to the westward, surrounding the island of Santa Catalina, which, with its canons and ravines, is as plainly visible as though viewed from its shore. The white sails on the water prove that life is even there, and the shipping in the harbor of San Pedro refutes the charge of no commerce from Southern California.

"Justly can it be claimed that the Sierra Madre foot-hills are the healthiest places to be found in Southern California, and therefore, may it be said, that, as Southern California is in to be the Sanitarium of the World, these slopes can not be equaled in the world for health. The air is

dry without being debilitating, warm in winter and mild in summer; no cold, damp fogs nor scorching winds, neither impure air nor impure water to poison the system that needs all its power, together with the best of climates, to regain its lost strength. No better place can be found for those afflicted with pulmonary difficulty. No place can equal these slopes for their life giving air. Much more could be said of La Cañada Valley, together with the rest of the foot hills along the Sierra Madre Mountains, but this valley is especially favored because it is not exposed to the full force of the sea breeze, nor to the hot winds and "Northers" that sweep the slope farther to the east, for while the sea breeze in the day is cool and refreshing, it is broken in force by the intervening Verdugo hills, which it has to cross reaching the valley, and the point of mountain that juts out into the plain to the east prevents the hot east winds from coming in, and sends them veering off towards the south. So, being thus sheltered, the invalid need fear nothing from the climate. The invigorating atmosphere, infusing new life into him, gives new being, and sickness meets an adversary which it finds hard to conquer.

La Canada, F.D. Lanterman, Agent, Room 7, Allen Block, Los Angeles."

Bibliography

Bonney, Richard E. *Beekeeping: A Practical Guide*. Pownal, VT: Storey Books, 1993.

Burdette, Robert B. *Greater Los Angeles & Southern California: Portraits & Personal Memorandum*. Chicago: Lewis Publishing Company, 1910.

Delaplane, Keith. *First Lessons in Beekeeping*. Hamilton, IL: Dadant Publishing, 2007.

Dougherty, June. *La Crescenta: Sources of History*. N.p.: self-published, 1993.

Farnsworth, R.W. *A Southern California Paradise, in the Suburbs of Los Angeles: Being a Historic and Descriptive Account of Pasadena, San Gabriel, Sierra Madre, and La Cañada*. Pasadena, CA: R.W. Farnsworth, 1883.

González, Michael J. *This Small City Will Be a Mexican Paradise.* Albuquerque: University of New Mexico Press, 2005.

La Cañada Presbyterian Church. *The First Hundred Years.* La Cañada Flintridge, CA: self-published, 1985.

Langstroth, L.L. *Langstroth's Hive and the Honey-Bee*. Philadelphia: L.B. Lippincott & Company, 1878.

Lawler, Mike, and Robert Newcombe. *La Crescenta: Images of America.* Charleston, SC: Arcadia Publishing, 2006.

Lombard, Sarah R. *Rancho Tujunga: A History of Sunland/Tujunga California.* N.p.: Bridge Publishing, 1990.

McGroaty, John Steven. *History of Los Angeles County*. Vol. 3. Chicago: American Historical Society Inc., 1925.

Montrose–Verdugo City Chamber of Commerce. *Montrose, California: The First Eighty Years*. Montrose, CA: self-published, 1993.

Oberbeck, Grace J. "A History of La Crescenta and La Cañada Valleys." *Crescenta Valley Ledger*, 1938.

Pate, Charles. *Reminisces of a Tenderfoot and Other Writings*. N.p.: Lanterman Historical Museum Foundation, 2014. The previously referenced manuscript was just published in a large paperback format in the past month.

Pinney, Joyce Y. *A Pasadena Chronology, 1769–1977*. Pasadena, CA: Pasadena Public Library, 1978.

Pomeroy, Elizabeth. *Lost and Found Historic Landmarks of the San Gabriel Valley*. Pasadena, CA: Many Moons Press, 2000.

Robinson, John W. *The San Gabriels*. Vol. 2. Arcadia, CA: Big Santa Anita Historical Society, 1983.

———. *Trails of the Angeles*. Berkeley, CA: Wilderness Press, 2008.

Robinson, W.W. *The Forest and the People: The Story of the Angeles National Forest*. Los Angeles: Title Insurance & Trust Company, 1946.

Root, A.J. *The ABC of Bee Culture*. Medina, OH: self-published, 1895.

Ungermann-Marshall, Yana. *Flintridge: Images of America*. Charleston, SC: Arcadia Publishing, 2008.

About the Author

Jo Anne Sadler is the author of *Crescenta Valley Pioneers and Their Legacies* and is currently president of the Historical Society of the Crescenta Valley. Her long-term interest in family history and immigration led her to being active in the historical society and researching the nineteenth-century history of the Crescenta Valley and the San Gabriel foothills.